WIRED FOR WEALTH

Change the Money Mindsets That Keep You Trapped and Unleash Your Wealth Potential

BRAD KLONTZ, PSY.D., TED KLONTZ, PH.D., AND RICK KAH

Health Communications, Inc.
Deerfield Beach, Florida

www.hcibooks.com

**Library of Congress Cataloging-in-Publication Data
is available through the Library of Congress.**

©2008 Brad Klontz, Ted Klontz, and Rick Kahler
ISBN-13: 978-0-7573-0794-2
ISBN-10: 0-7573-0794-9

The names, locations, and other identifying information of the individuals in this book have been changed to protect their privacy. This book contains general information and is not intended to be, nor should it be, used as a substitute for specific medical or psychological advice.

Publisher: Health Communications, Inc.
   3201 S.W. 15th Street
   Deerfield Beach, FL 33442-8190

Cover design by Justin Rotkowitz
Interior design and formatting by Dawn Von Strolley Grove

CONTENTS

————————— ❦ —————————

ACKNOWLEDGMENTS

—————⟨⟩—————

We would like to acknowledge the many people who have supported and continue to support our work. Special thanks first to our spouses: Joni Wada, Margie Zugich, and Marcia Kahler. Without your love, patience, encouragement, and support, this book would not have been possible.

Brad also thanks family members Wanda and James Turner and John and Diane Wada for their ongoing encouragement. Ted appreciates daughter Brenda for handling the all-so-important day-to-day issues, as well as granddaughter Morgan, daughter-in-law Joni, and son-in-law Antoine for their vision and support. Rick is grateful for daughter London and son Davin, who are amazing and the light of his life. He thanks his loyal associates, Darla Creal and Lindsay Luper, for keeping his financial planning clients fully supported and cared for.

Thanks also to the many financial planners, coaches, therapists, and clients we have worked with and learned from over the years. You have been our greatest teachers. We are grateful to our editor, Kathleen Fox, for her contributions, conscientiousness, and hard work. Thanks to Dr. Alex Bivens for his assistance in analyzing our survey data. Thanks also to the great staff at Health Communications, Inc., including Peter Vegso, Gary Seidler, Allison Janse, and Kim Weiss.

We also want to acknowledge and honor one another. Our partnership, shared vision, and commitment have helped us forge a new path in integrating financial planning and psychology, and our friendship continues to enrich our lives.

INTRODUCTION

---◦◦◦---

W*hat's the formula* for achieving wealth?

While we can learn much by studying the methods of people who have achieved wealth, many successful people would have difficulty telling you exactly what they did that made the difference. They just worked long hours, kept trying, didn't give up, and made it big. Everyone is different, and it can be very difficult to replicate someone else's method of achieving success.

Although the "secret" to achieving wealth can't be distilled into a tidy one-size-fits-all formula, the truth is that people who are wealthy think and act differently from those who are not. And in fact, there are discernable patterns of beliefs and behaviors about money that are associated with wealth, and there are patterns that are associated with poverty and financial chaos. These patterns represent your "money mindsets," or the ways you think about money and your resulting actions.

The exciting news is that you *can change* your money mindsets. If your pattern of thinking about money is associated with destructive financial behaviors, financial distress, and poverty, you can change that pattern to one that is associated with wealth. Regardless of your starting point or your financial situation, you can quite literally *rewire your brain for wealth*. This book shows you how.

Changing your money mindsets is not a gimmick. It is a process, based on psychological principles and research, to help you identify and change your mental and emotional blocks to success. While this process is intended to help you make money, it will also help you achieve authentic wealth. Certainly, having enough money is a fundamental part of authentic wealth. However, studies consistently show what we know in our hearts to be true: money and material possessions alone bring nothing more than the most fleeting happiness. Providing well for your family, being able to have and do the things that matter to you, and enjoying financial security are all important. Following the advice and completing the exercises in this book will help you remove the barriers that keep you from becoming rich.

Equally important, however, is the ability to use financial wealth to support a balanced, fulfilling, passionate life. Financial success is only one of the many benefits that can come from changing your money mindsets. A change in mindsets will also allow you to enjoy the wealth you may already have. Rewiring the money beliefs that block your financial potential can lead to wiser financial choices, more balance in your life concerning money, improved relationships, and increased wealth and financial comfort.

As important as these benefits are, changing your money mindsets can transform your life in even more significant ways. This is due to the incredible consequences of money-related stress. When money is a source of stress, that stress influences every aspect of your life. Recent research has shown that stress about money issues affects not only your mental state but also your physical health. A June 2008 poll conducted by the Associated Press suggests that stress about money matters is an important health factor. People who worried about money reported more migraines, ulcers, anxiety, and incidences of severe depression. You have limited control over many external factors that affect your financial environment (for example, job loss, recession, high-tech bubble burst, subprime mortgage crunch). What you *can* control, however, are your own thoughts and subsequent actions (or inaction) within that environment. In our clinical, professional, and personal experience, these internal factors will be the major determinant of your ultimate success.

Accepting your role—and the fact that you have one—in your financial situation is the first step in ensuring that you don't continue to make the same mistakes. Using the tools in this book, you can examine and learn to change the beliefs you have about money that are not serving you well. You can learn how to rewire your beliefs to set you on a path to financial success and less money stress.

Wired for Wealth is based on a combination of hands-on experience and research. We are pioneers in the practical application of the psychology of personal finance and wealth. Dr. Brad Klontz is a clinical psychologist, psychotherapist, and researcher. Dr. Ted Klontz has been a psychotherapist and life coach for more than thirty-five years. Rick Kahler has been a fee-only certified financial planner for twenty-five years. We all work with clients on a daily basis, and together we have decades of experience in helping clients to build wealth, change self-limiting patterns of behavior, and create more fulfilling lives.

Much of the work in the emerging field of neuroeconomics, which combines the fields of psychology and finance, focuses on laboratory studies that identify the common mental errors that people make. This research is then applied to helping people make better investing decisions. Much of this research has been expertly reviewed by Jason Zweig in his groundbreaking book *Your Money and Your Mind.*

Wired for Wealth goes far beyond specific investing advice and mental tricks. Our goal is for you to entirely transform your relationship with money so it becomes a generous partner that works to support your goals. Rather than reviewing the common mental errors of investors, our tested transformational exercises give you an intimate opportunity to examine and change your unique limiting money mindsets.

For this book, we also did something quite novel in the field of wealth coaching: we conducted research. Rather than hypothesizing what a wealthy mindset is or just giving you our opinion about what has worked for us and our clients, we researched the money beliefs and behaviors of those with wealth and those without. Our goal was to learn what, if anything, distinguished their thinking from one another. We found a clear connection between beliefs and wealth, with some surprising results.

Although financial education, positive thinking, and positive visualization are all valuable, these techniques are just the beginning, rather than the end, of the process of rewiring our brains for wealth. For most of us, information is just not enough to change our behaviors. For example, we all know that we should save for the future and not spend more than we make. Nevertheless, in recent years Americans have accumulated a great deal of personal debt and have saved very little. Although we know better, we are obviously not doing what we know we should do.

In many cases, there is a block to putting your knowledge into action. Until you confront this barrier, change is not likely to happen. The barrier consists not only of self-limiting statements and beliefs but also of social, family, and psychological issues. To address this gap, we developed a change process that integrates the fields of financial planning and financial psychology to help people reduce their financial stress and improve their financial health. The integration of expertise in these two fields sets our work apart from the typical financial advice.

Our transformative work was first featured in Jeff Zaslow's "Moving On" column in the *The Wall Street Journal* in 2003.

Since then, it has received a great deal of attention in the fields of finance and psychology, and it has been featured in several media sources, including NBC's *Today* show, National Public Radio, *The New York Times*, *The Washington Post*, *Money* magazine, and *Good Morning America*.

Our process of transformation is more than a theory. We have observed the successful transformation of many clients, including those whose stories have been adapted for this book. We also conducted scientific research on whether people actually change after going through a money makeover process. This clinical outcome study, conducted from 2004 to 2006, was one of the first to involve changing a client's money beliefs and behaviors.

The study evaluated people who participated in financial therapy through a process, similar to the one described in this book, of rewiring their money mindsets by identifying their money beliefs, examining their financial patterns, exploring their past experiences with money, and rewriting their money beliefs. These individuals experienced significant and lasting positive changes, including improvements in mood, decreased anxiety about money, and improvements in overall financial and psychological health. The study was published in the August 2008 edition of *Psychological Services*, a journal of the American Psychological Association.

Our latest research involves a comprehensive study of money beliefs and financial behaviors that we conducted from May to July 2008. We examined the beliefs and behaviors of 422 people from all walks of life, income levels, and levels of net worth. Here are some general statistics about the participants:

- The age range was eighteen to eighty, with 70 percent between the ages of thirty-one and sixty.
- Women made up 65 percent of the group, and men made up 35 percent.
- Most had a bachelor's degree or higher.
- Most were employed full-time by someone else or were self-employed.
- Yearly income ranged from less than $10,000 to more than $1 million.
- Net worth ranged from less than zero (owing more money than the total worth of one's assets) to more than $10 million.
- Credit card debt from the previous month was carried by 40 percent.
- More than $10,000 in credit card debt from the previous month was carried by 10 percent.
- Bankruptcy had been filed for by 7 percent at some time in the past.
- In terms of socioeconomic status, 40 percent were raised in middle-class families, 32 percent were raised in lower-middle-class or working-class families, 21 percent were raised in upper-middle-class families, 5 percent were raised in poor families, and 2 percent were raised in wealthy families.

- In terms of home ownership, 54 percent owned a home with a mortgage, 18 percent owned a home without a mortgage, and 19 percent were renting.
- In terms of marital status, 56 percent were married, 8 percent were not married but were living with a significant other, 20 percent had never married, and 16 percent were separated, divorced, or widowed.

This survey revealed some striking differences between the beliefs of the wealthy and of those who struggle financially. We also found some major differences in beliefs and behavior between men and women and between younger adults and older adults—some of which might not bode well for either the retiring baby boomers or the up-and-coming boomerang generation. This is hardly surprising, given the recent rapid rise in consumerism, the easy availability of consumer credit, and our current "have to have it now" culture.

Throughout this book, we'll deconstruct the mindsets of the wealthy and the poor, and we'll teach you to rewire your way of thinking about money. Using real client examples, we'll show you how to identify your harmful money patterns, and we'll offer you tools to give yourself a financial health makeover.

Before you read further, we encourage you to take the money beliefs self-test at the beginning of Chapter 1. Your answers will reveal whether your thinking about money more closely matches the thinking of those who are wealthy or those who are not. As our study results demonstrate, successful people and unsuccessful people have different patterns of thinking about money. Your thoughts and beliefs about money do have a significant impact on your financial health and your potential for achieving wealth and success. We will show you not only how you formed your money beliefs but also how you can rewire those beliefs and form new patterns that will help you to bring authentic wealth and abundance into your life.

CHAPTER ONE

THE SCIENCE AND PSYCHOLOGY OF MONEY SCRIPTS

*P*lease take a few minutes to complete the questionnaire that follows, which is taken from the survey we used in our research. Each item listed is a "money script," or a belief about money. Later in the book, you'll have the opportunity to compare your answers to our research findings. Your answers can reveal a great deal about your wealth potential.

Place an X in the box that best describes the extent to which you agree or disagree with each of the following statements. Please answer all the items.

MONEY SCRIPTS QUESTIONNAIRE

	Strongly Agree	Agree	Slightly Agree	Slightly Disagree	Disagree	Strongly Disagree
1. It is important to save for a rainy day.	❏	❏	❏	❏	❏	❏
2. Giving money to others is something people should do.	❏	❏	❏	❏	❏	❏
3. Money buys freedom.	❏	❏	❏	❏	❏	❏
4. I have to work hard to be sure I have enough money.	❏	❏	❏	❏	❏	❏
5. I deserve money.	❏	❏	❏	❏	❏	❏
6. Your self-worth equals your net worth.	❏	❏	❏	❏	❏	❏

	Strongly Agree	Agree	Slightly Agree	Slightly Disagree	Disagree	Strongly Disagree
7. It is okay to keep secrets from your partner around money.	❏	❏	❏	❏	❏	❏
8. More money will make you happier.	❏	❏	❏	❏	❏	❏
9. I do not deserve a lot of money when others have less than I do.	❏	❏	❏	❏	❏	❏
10. I will never be able to afford the things I really want in life.	❏	❏	❏	❏	❏	❏
11. Things would get better if I had more money.	❏	❏	❏	❏	❏	❏
12. If you are good, your financial needs will be taken care of.	❏	❏	❏	❏	❏	❏
13. It takes money to make money.	❏	❏	❏	❏	❏	❏
14. If I had to borrow money to get what I want, I would do it.	❏	❏	❏	❏	❏	❏
15. You can't trust people around money.	❏	❏	❏	❏	❏	❏

Now that you have a sense of some of your own beliefs about money, let's explore the concept of money scripts.

MONEY SCRIPTS

Natalie would be the first to tell you, "I'm just not good with money." She manages to pay her rent, utilities, and car payment every month, but the payments are frequently late. She uses her debit card for everything else, running up overdraft charges nearly every month because she has no idea how much money is in her account. One of her dresser drawers is full of unopened bank statements.

As a licensed practical nurse, Natalie earns enough money to live comfortably, yet she always seems to find herself in the middle of another financial crisis. Her car was recently impounded—the consequence of ignoring a year's worth of parking tickets. It made her sick to have to ask her parents to pay the tickets, the impoundment fees, and the hefty fine to get her car back. The total cost was nearly as much as her car was worth. Her parents sent her a check, along with a four-page letter scolding her for being so stupid. She was further humiliated by having to make a court appearance and listen to a lecture from the judge. As soon as it was over, she went to the mall and bought two new pairs of shoes. Shopping always seems to make Natalie feel better.

Like Natalie, many of us aren't managing money well. Americans have record-high debt and record-low savings rates—we are among the worst of all the developed countries. This isn't because we lack the income. On a global basis, we have one of the highest earnings per capita. Nevertheless, with an average savings rate in 2005 of *minus* 0.5 percent—the lowest since the Great Depression—the average American spends more money than he or she makes. According to a report by the Department of Labor, a 2005 study done by Sharon DeVaney and Sophia Chiremba of Perdue University found that 19 percent of the respondents had spent more than their income, and 56 percent of the baby boomers usually spend all of—or more than—what they earn.

Clearly, many Americans are in bad financial shape. However, the basics of financial health are actually quite simple: spend less than you make and invest the difference for the future. Few of us can honestly say that we don't know we should live within our means, save for a rainy day, and fund a retirement plan. Someone like Natalie would be quick to acknowledge that she should have a budget, pay more attention to her finances, spend less, and save more.

Since we know what we should do to manage money more wisely, why are so few of us doing it? If our behavior with money causes us so much stress, why don't we just do what we know we should do? Natalie is a smart woman. Why can't she learn from her expensive mistakes and humiliation and behave more responsibly with her money? It doesn't make sense to keep making the same destructive financial choices over and over when we know we should stop.

In reality, however, our self-defeating actions do make sense. Even the most self-destructive financial behaviors make perfect sense when we understand what drives those behaviors. All our decisions and actions or inaction concerning money, including those that do not serve us well, are based, with perfect logic, on our beliefs about money. These beliefs are called *money scripts*.

Money scripts are the thoughts, beliefs, and attitudes that we hold about money. Many of our associations with money are hidden deeply in the unconscious mind. The new field of neuroeconomics combines the sciences of psychology and economics to identify how these patterns of thinking and emotions affect financial decisions.

For example, research conducted by Hersh Shefrin and Meir Statman of the University of Santa Clara and published in the *Journal of Finance* (1985) showed that people do not trade stocks in a rational manner. They found that people have a natural disposition to sell winning stocks too early and hold onto losing stocks too long. In this study, only a minority of stock trades occurred in accordance with rational principles, because people tried to avoid feeling regret by not selling losing stocks, sought feelings of pride by selling stocks that were winning, and had difficulty with self-control.

Similar studies show that the average human being suffers

from thinking errors and emotions that affect investing decisions. Psychologists and financial coaches know that each of
our brains is individually wired to think certain ways about
money based on our personal experiences with money.

Our money scripts affect every decision we make that directly
or indirectly involves money. These scripts are formed during
childhood and are further developed and shaped through our
life experiences. We don't even realize that we believe these
"truths" about money—what it is, what it can do, and how it
works. We are taught that it is not polite to talk about money.
Thus, we keep our beliefs to ourselves and do not open our
thinking to new awareness or understanding. Conscious or not,
money scripts define our relationship with money and lie at the
foundation of all our financial behaviors.

WHERE DO MONEY SCRIPTS COME FROM?

As children, we internalize the messages we receive from our
surroundings and integrate that information to help us make sense
of the world. We receive messages, both overtly and covertly, from
our parents, other significant people in our lives, our life circumstances, and society as a whole. Just as children depend on their
parents to provide nourishing food, they also depend on the adults
in their lives to provide nourishing, accurate information and messages about the world. Many of those messages are about money.

Many money scripts come from beliefs that are spoken or otherwise directly communicated to us by some authority figure. For example, parents might pay children for chores or require them to save part of their allowances. They might directly tell children such things as "Money can't buy happiness," "It's just as easy to fall in love with a rich man as a poor one," "Money doesn't grow on trees," or "Spend your money on education; nobody can ever take that away from you." Children may also simply overhear Mom and Dad say those things to others.

Other money scripts are indirect; they come from beliefs that we internalize from listening to other people or watching their behavior, from seeing the way that rich and poor people are regarded and portrayed in the media, and from absorbing thoughts, feelings, and behaviors concerning money from our parents.

Children whose parents worry about money, for example, may grow up to be insecure and fearful about finances. Those whose parents are envious of wealthy people and resentful about their own circumstances may develop money scripts such as "Being rich is the most important thing in life," "Rich people are shallow," or "If you're poor, it's somebody else's fault." If these beliefs are not identified, explored, and modified, the children who are exposed to them will grow up to unconsciously communicate the same messages to their own children.

Because children take in and process messages about money

in individual ways, the money scripts they learn from their situations can vary. Two children from the same family can grow up with different worldviews about money and totally different adaptations.

The deepest and most stubborn money scripts come from circumstances or events that are associated with strong emotional or traumatic experiences. The actual role that money plays in the event is less important than its association. The more primitive part of our brain, whose primary purpose is to help us survive, often misinterprets the significance that money has played in a particularly traumatic situation. To protect us from further emotional harm, the primitive brain's association between money and pain can lead us to unconscious actions that end up hurting our financial health but have no survival value.

For example, a child growing up in a wealthy family in which there is a significant amount of emotional pain might associate money with family dysfunction. In reality, money does not cause dysfunction, but its misuse can be a symptom of an underlying dysfunction (for example, divorce, abuse, alcoholism). However, an unconsciously held negative association involving money can lead to deeply held money scripts and can lead a person to "choosing" a life of avoiding wealth. Conversely, a child who grows up in a poor family in which there is substantial emotional pain might erroneously associate the pain with a lack of money. This child may then engage in a

workaholic life of pursuing money at the expense of relationships, health, or spiritual development, believing that money
will bring love, connection, and joy.

Sometimes the significance of money-related traumatic associations and events is readily apparent: the parents losing a business or going through bankruptcy, being evicted from the
family home, intense family conflict about money, or a parent
being incarcerated for embezzlement. At other times, events
might seem unimportant but can still result in deeply embed-
ded money scripts because children attach such strong emotion
to them. For example, a child may want something that the
family can't afford. The parents' saying no may be done in a
way that the child interprets as deeply shaming. To avoid experiencing such shame in the future, the child might develop a
money script of "It's wrong to want anything." This could
result in a life of unnecessarily denying comforts and pleasures
to oneself and perhaps one's family.

Our money scripts may be exact copies of our parents' teach-
ings and actions about money. Thus we may find ourselves, for
better or worse, creating the same financial situation our parents created. For example, a boy raised in poverty may incorporate a money script of "No matter what I do, I will always be
poor." If left unchallenged, such a belief could lead him to a
life of underachievement in which he ignores opportunities to
create wealth and interprets financial defeat as a confirmation
of his sorry lot in life. On the other hand, a boy raised in a

wealthy family might have the money script "I am meant to be rich," resulting in a dogged pursuit of wealth. When he experiences a setback, he might shake it off or chalk it up as a learning experience, being convinced that wealth is his birthright. In adulthood, both boys will unconsciously create the destiny they believe is theirs, and those around them will join them in those beliefs and respond to them in kind.

However, it is also common to form money scripts that are the opposite of what our parents do, often as a reaction against our parents' way of doing things. When strong feelings are involved, we might adopt an opposite and equally unbalanced and destructive belief, even if it is not good for us. For example, Charlie, the son of a workaholic father who still hurts from his father's absence in his life, decided that "the pursuit of money is bad—look what it cost me." This money script resulted in an exaggerated desire to avoid work, leading to a life of unnecessary poverty and underachievement for Charlie and his family.

Shelly, the daughter of a single mother on welfare whose choices were limited, decided that "money is the most important thing" and organized her life to maximize her ability to earn. That money script essentially cost her own daughter and son their mother; Shelly was rarely around because she worked so much. History is full of such rags-to-riches stories, illustrating the ability of people like Shelly to step out of their natal family's financial legacy by adopting money scripts that are more conducive to acquiring and increasing wealth. The family they create as adults often pays the price for such a single-minded pursuit.

Money scripts that result from traumatic or deeply emotional experiences are formed at a deep, primal level and become part of our worldview. These beliefs, developed for survival and protection in an unpredictable world, are often incredibly strong, resistant to change, and totally unconscious.

Natalie, whom we introduced at the beginning of this chapter, had a money script of "I'm not good with money" that was created when she was a little girl. Her mother was a nurse and her father was the bookkeeper for a large law firm. As the family's "money expert," he paid the bills and made the financial decisions. The only discussions Natalie ever heard about money consisted of her father lecturing her mother about not keeping to the budget.

When Natalie and her sister were old enough to receive allowances, they had to account to their father every week for what they spent. If he didn't approve of their choices, he told them they wouldn't get any money the next week. By the end of the week, he always relented and gave them the money, with an accompanying lecture. Natalie soon learned to avoid the lecture by lying about her spending. She also learned that in a pinch she could go to her mother, who would give her additional money without her father's knowledge.

Some of the money scripts Natalie developed were "I'm too stupid to learn to manage money," "Money matters are the man's province," "My parents will always lecture me, but they'll always bail me out," and "Money is used to manipulate others." These beliefs were internalized, and Natalie organized her entire financial life around them, as if they were absolute truths. Natalie's money scripts make perfect sense, given where she came from. As long as they go unrecognized and unchallenged, however, they will continue to limit her ability to achieve financial health.

MONEY SCRIPTS ARE PARTIAL TRUTHS

A money script is not necessarily wrong, but neither is it necessarily right. Our scripts are often skewed, exaggerated, or one-dimensional, consisting of incomplete or partial truths. They are usually highly contextual, true in one circumstance but false in many others.

Take, for example, the money script "Money can't buy happiness." Certainly this is true, in the right circumstances. Having wealth doesn't guarantee a satisfying, fulfilling life. So in that circumstance, money can't buy happiness. The money script is also false—but again, it depends on the circumstance. For example, being in poverty, struggling to provide necessities, and having no financial security, can be a stressful and an unhappy way to live. Research shows that in that situation, having more money could indeed provide an increased level of happiness.

Many money scripts make sense and are appropriate for the original circumstances that shape them. For example, Natalie's money script, "My parents will always lecture me, but they'll always bail me out," would be a valid belief as long as her parents are alive, their financial circumstances allow them to help her, and they are willing to continue to rescue her from her financial predicaments. However, suppose that after the parking-ticket fiasco, her parents decide that it's time she learned to be more responsible. The next time she asks for help, they say no. Suppose her parents retire or need money for unexpected medical expenses and no longer have enough money to help her.

The reason they stop helping Natalie isn't important. What matters is that if she has learned to count on getting money from them and that money is no longer there, her money script no longer works. Yet since the belief lies on an unconscious level, the chances are that she will continue to follow it long after it is accurate. She will get into trouble, appeal to her parents for help, and not know what to do when that help is not forthcoming. She and her parents may have a huge fight that damages their relationship. Her parents could give in, putting their own financial security at risk. Maybe Natalie will find someone else, perhaps a boyfriend, to take care of her financially. Perhaps in an unconscious way Natalie finds a new parent, "Mom Master Card" or "Dad Visa," who plays the financial role her parents once filled. No matter what the outcome, it will almost certainly result in stress and pain, both financially and emotionally.

Since most of us have scores of money scripts, some of them might contradict one another. For example, Allen was raised to believe that "Rich people are greedy and selfish." At the same time, he got the message loud and clear from the culture around him that "Success is measured by how much you earn." Such conflicting money scripts can contribute to one's stress about money and lead to immobility. As Allen put it, "I'm damned if I do and damned if I don't." Conflicting money scripts can also keep someone like Allen on a financial roller coaster of making lots of money only to find ways to financially sabotage himself when he is successful.

Since our money scripts are mostly unconscious, we don't question their accuracy or examine the degree to which they are true and work for us, yet we continue to act on them as if they were entirely true. We follow them blindly, even when they no longer fit our circumstances and even when they cause pain in our lives. Because we have no idea of the beliefs behind our money choices, we might blame our financial difficulties and pain on other people and external circumstances, locking ourselves into a cycle of financial stress and self-destructive behaviors, feeling victimized and powerless. Because we don't talk to others about money, we have little opportunity to have these beliefs challenged.

---◦◦◦---

CHAPTER TWO

THE TOP TEN MONEY SCRIPTS THAT MESS UP PEOPLE'S FINANCIAL LIVES

We have identified a "top ten" list of the money scripts we see in our work with people who are suffering from chronic financial stress. These money scripts represent categories of beliefs that are associated with problematic financial situations, lower income, and lower net worth. If left unchallenged, these money scripts will contribute to some of the most common self-destructive and self-limiting financial behaviors that people exhibit.

1. "MORE MONEY WILL MAKE THINGS BETTER."

This is perhaps one of the most common money scripts for Americans. We set arbitrary "more money" targets, believing that those magical numbers will bring us meaning, peace, happiness, security, or whatever else we seek. The problem is that when the target is met, the corresponding payoff never quite seems to show up. So we look for more, becoming like a donkey in pursuit of a tempting carrot just out of reach: no matter how fast we run, we never quite get there. Entire lives, even generations of lives, can be dedicated to the pursuit of the fulfillment of this money script.

As a young man, Monte was sure that when he had enough money he would be happy. In his thirties he said, "If I had a net worth of $500,000, I would be happy." By the time he was in his forties, doing well in a small service business, his "happiness target" had increased to $1 million. In his midsixties, he retired and sold the business, ending up with more than $2 million.

When a friend congratulated him on his success, he said, "Yes, but I really wanted to get another $300,000 out of it. Then I would be happy."

Certainly, up to a point, there is some truth in this money script. If someone is barely scraping by from one paycheck to the next on a limited income, more money would indeed make things better. Once we are able to comfortably take care of our needs, however, happiness is not related to the amount of money we have. Research shows that there is no significant correlation between more money and increased happiness once a household's income is above $50,000 per year. If people have enough money to be comfortable, but they aren't happy, they will probably still be unhappy at a higher income level. A 1987 *Chicago Tribune* poll found that those who made $30,000 per year believed that a yearly income of $50,000 would make them happy, whereas those who made $100,000 were convinced that $250,000 would satisfy their needs.

One recent lottery winner, when asked during an interview what it would mean to him now that he had won more than $124 million, said, "It won't change me, but I can tell you one thing for sure, my daughter will be happy the rest of her life." If he never modifies this money script, we suspect that he and his daughter might both experience some significant pain at some point because of this belief.

In our study, the belief that more money will make things better or bring happiness was associated not with high income or net worth but with compulsive hoarding, workaholism, financial denial, overspending, and underemployment. This belief was also endorsed significantly more by those ages twenty to forty than those ages fifty to eighty.

2. "MONEY IS BAD."

Like all money scripts, this one has many variations, including such beliefs as "The rich are shallow, greedy, insensitive, and/or unhappy"; "The rich got that way by taking advantage of others"; and "When money walks in the front door, love walks out the back door." Anyone who operates from this unconscious money script is likely to unwittingly sabotage any potential financial progress. After all, if you believe that having money makes people bad or unhappy, it is perfectly logical that you would find it hard to work toward accumulating any. It is also logical that you might reject or try to get rid of money that came your way.

Darren, for example, is in his late twenties and has a dream of using his talent as a poet to help children understand other cultures. He lives and travels in an old minivan, giving away a book of poems he has self-published, teaching a free class he has developed, and living on donations and the kindness of strangers. He talks with pride about his ability to live on almost nothing and his commitment to simplicity. He doesn't mention that his wealthy family gave him $250,000 to fund his project. He has spent most of the money much faster than necessary, getting rid of it by choosing the most expensive options for printing his books and hiring a high-priced but ineffective publicist. He says, "Money will taint my soul and kill my poetry."

In our study, the younger generation, especially people between the ages of eighteen and twenty-five, endorsed negative views about money and the rich significantly more than their elders did. For example, when compared to those above fifty years old, they were more likely to agree that "People get rich by taking advantage of others," "Rich people are greedy," and "Money is the root of all evil." At this time we are uncertain whether these beliefs are age-related—that is, typical for past generations also—or whether they represent only this generation's way of thinking about money. It is important to note that the younger generation has significantly less income and net worth, which is to be expected, but this generation also exhibits significantly more overspending and compulsive spending behaviors.

3. "I DON'T DESERVE MONEY."

This money script is held by many people who have received sums of money, such as inheritances or insurance payouts, that they didn't earn or don't fully accept as their own. It also appears in people who have accumulated money through their own efforts but who believe that they should not enjoy what money can give them because others are not so fortunate. It is a common script for those in the helping professions. This money script is often associated with low self-esteem. It can keep people emotionally and spiritually poor despite any wealth they might have. Those with this belief tend to earn less than they are capable of and to make ill-advised financial decisions. Both these behaviors are unconscious attempts to get rid of what they don't believe they deserve.

In her late forties, Sherri, a high school teacher and divorced mother of two teenagers, inherited several hundred thousand dollars from her father. Instead of paying off her mortgage or investing the inheritance for her future, she took her children on a cruise and donated $100,000 to a local charity. She bought a new BMW, and throughout the next few years she traded it in for a newer one every time a new model came out. Sherri told a friend, "My father always thought I was a loser who couldn't handle money. He only left me this as a way to keep trying to control me from his grave. I won't have any peace until that money is gone."

4. "I DESERVE TO SPEND MONEY."

Like all money scripts, this one contains a partial truth. One aspect of financial balance is believing that we deserve to spend money on ourselves, on those close to us, and on those less fortunate. However, this script can undermine our financial health when it is used as a rationale for borrowing money or depleting retirement savings in order to buy things we don't need.

As a child, Carson saw his parents lose their business, their savings, and the family home as a result of his father's mis-management and high-risk investments. As an adult, Carson routinely spent everything he earned as fast as he got it. His belief was "I might as well spend it before someone else takes it away from me."

5. "THERE WILL NEVER BE ENOUGH MONEY."

Ebenezer Scrooge, the miser described by Charles Dickens in *A Christmas Carol,* is a classic example of this money script at its most extreme. When we believe that there will never be enough money, we set ourselves up to live a life of deprivation and to experience constant anxiety, insecurity, and fear. Workaholics who neglect their relationships, their children, and their health may operate from this money script. The same is true for those who grew up in poverty. Although this belief might partially serve us by fostering drive, ambition, and a solid work ethic, it can also keep us from enjoying the benefits of that hard work.

Steven and Linda, a police officer and a medical administrator, respectively, lived modestly and invested for their future. At sixty, they retired with a $2 million investment portfolio. Their plan was to live on their retirement pensions and the income from their investments, which would give them more than enough to live comfortably and do the traveling they had always wanted to do. Yet a few months into retirement, both of them discovered that they were terrified of losing the security represented by their $2 million. Linda got a part-time job as an office manager, and Steven began selling home security systems. This allowed them to avoid taking any income out of their portfolio, but it ended their dream of doing the things they had hoped to do when they retired.

6. "THERE WILL ALWAYS BE ENOUGH MONEY."

This money script drives the behaviors of many people who grew up in wealthy families, because they could always count on having enough money to do or have anything they wanted. It also may apply to people who have always been taken care of financially by someone else. This script could even have its origin in families with little or no financial security, if the parents assumed that "something will always show up" to take care of needs as they arose. This money script reflects an unconscious trust that the universe will always take care of us, regardless of our actions or inaction.

Barry and his brother, who had grown up in a wealthy family, were partners in a dealership specializing in high-end boats. When their local economy hit hard times, the business was facing failure. Barry told his accountant that he had decided to sign his share in the business over to his brother and walk away, with no attempt to revamp the business to get through the hard times, no provisions to recover any of his investment in the business, and no prospect for another job in a depressed employment market. He was already having trouble paying his day-to-day bills. When his accountant protested that this action was foolish, Barry said, "Don't worry, it's only money. I'll just make some more."

7. "MONEY IS UNIMPORTANT."

This money script is common for people who are in the helping professions, who are creative artists, or who have religious beliefs that poverty is required to achieve virtue. It can grow out of the belief that wealth doesn't bring happiness, love, or belonging. It allows people to excuse and rationalize poor financial planning, lack of concern about financial matters, lack of ambition, and sometimes even laziness.

Despite an engineering degree that qualified her for a financially successful career, by the time she was fifty years old, Joy was working as a waitress, had no savings, and owned nothing except a fifteen-year-old car that was a gift from her brother. She had been married and divorced three times and declared bankruptcy twice. Every time she came close to achieving even minimal financial success, Joy would take what she had accumulated and volunteer for another charitable project that consumed both her time and her savings. She believed that her calling was to help others and that paying attention to her own financial security would somehow betray or stifle that calling.

8. "MONEY WILL GIVE MY LIFE MEANING."

This money script may result from growing up in poverty and seeing money as a magic tool that can open doors to belonging or being treated with respect. It can also be tied to a belief that money is the primary measure of success. Many people who have this money script will vehemently deny it, instead reciting a contradictory money script, "Everyone knows that money can't give you meaning in life." However, an examination of their behaviors shows that they are operating from a belief that money will give them meaning.

Eliot, whose ambition and intelligence helped him to escape from a childhood of poverty and abuse, spent his career building a business that made him both a multimillionaire and a legend in his field. In his sixties, he realized that his intense drive toward financial success had come at a tremendous cost. He said to us, "I have all the money and fame any one person could want. Yet I don't have any real friends, and my kids hate me. I thought that money would help me find peace and love, but it didn't. I don't have any idea of what I want the most, and even if I did, I wouldn't know where to start to get it."

9. "IT'S NOT NICE (OR NECESSARY) TO TALK ABOUT MONEY."

This script is very common in our culture. We are inundated with books, magazines, radio shows, and television programs about earning and managing money. Yet talking about money *and our relationship to it* is one of our biggest taboos. It is easier for us to talk about our sexual secrets than our money secrets. The subject of money—how much we earn, what we believe about it, how we relate to it, and how we behave with it—is in many ways the biggest and most shameful secret in American life.

Bryanna had this money script driven home in an unforgettable way. When she was about eight, she asked her mother one day how much money her father made. Her mother slapped her in the face and said, "Don't you ever mention money in this home again!" Bryanna never asked another question about money—and it cost her dearly. When her dad gave her part of her inheritance early, he told her to take it to a certain investment advisor. She did so and did not ask any questions. Over the next seven years, the advisor managed to lose 80 percent of the money. Only after she got a notice from him that she had very little money left did she discover that not asking questions about money—her money, this time—had destroyed her financially.

10. "IF YOU ARE GOOD, THE UNIVERSE WILL SUPPLY ALL YOUR NEEDS."

This belief is especially common among those in the helping professions or with strong religious backgrounds. They believe that if they do all the right things for all the right reasons, then they won't have to worry about the future because their "good karma" will guarantee that good things will happen.

Beth took seriously her church's admonitions that she should not accumulate riches on earth, that it was more blessed to give than to receive, and that what she gave to others would be returned to her tenfold. She worked as a secretary at the church, tithing nearly half her salary even though she received far less than the prevailing wage for such work, and not worrying about the fact that no FICA (social security) taxes were withheld from her wages. In her seventies, when her health finally forced her to retire, she had nothing to live on.

CHANGING YOUR MONEY MINDSET: IDENTIFYING YOUR MONEY SCRIPTS

The questionnaire in Chapter 1 gave you a start on identifying your money scripts. The questions below will give you some additional insight. Take a few minutes to answer them on a separate piece of paper. Don't analyze the questions or think too much about your responses. Just write down the first thoughts that come to mind.

Some people contend that both Mother Teresa and Bill Gates have contributed to the betterment of humanity. Who do you think has made the most important contribution to society: Mother Teresa or Bill Gates?

Imagine that you walk into a room. On your left sits all the love and peace you and your loved ones could ever have. On your right sits all the money that you and your loved ones could ever use. What choice do you make? Why?

Complete the following sentences:

The wealthy got that way by _____

Retirement means _____

Poor people are poor because _____

I justify having more than I need by believing _____

The relationship between sex and money is _____

The relationship between God, spirituality, religion and money is

_____

Becoming *Wired for Wealth* is fundamentally a process of rewiring your money scripts. When you become aware of your money scripts, you have taken the first step to interrupt the unconscious and destructive cycle of acting automatically in response to money beliefs you don't even know you have. You become able to make money decisions based on your current circumstances and needs rather than on unconscious and incomplete "truths" about money that you learned in childhood.

These mostly unconscious money scripts are based on associations between money and strong emotions that are stored in the limbic, or more primitive, part of the human brain. This part of the brain operates without our conscious consent, especially in times of stress. However, because we learned these lessons, we can also unlearn them, by rewiring or retraining this part of the brain. In our work, we have seen numerous examples of dramatic changes that people have been able to make in their financial lives as a result of such rewiring.

If you have taken the time to complete the Chapter 1 questionnaire and the exercises above, you are probably beginning to identify some of your most prevalent money scripts. Keep them in mind as you read further. Look for patterns in your answers. Were you aware that you had these beliefs? How do you think they have affected your financial decisions? How do they fit with your values? Which ones are serving you well and which ones do you think might be limiting your financial potential? In later chapters, we provide ways to understand more clearly and begin to rewire those parts of your brain that control the money scripts that are limiting your success or keeping you stuck. Incorporating healthier money beliefs can lay a strong foundation for building financial health and abundance.

CHAPTER THREE

YOUR FINANCIAL COMFORT ZONE: DO YOU NEED TO BREAK OUT?

In what kind of neighborhood did you grow up? A suburb? An exclusive gated community? A high-rise apartment in an area marked by poverty? A culturally diverse middle-class city neighborhood? A small town? A farm? A ranch community?

Whatever your circumstances, you probably grew up in a neighborhood where the majority of the inhabitants were in many ways a lot like you. Just imagine one such neighborhood: a stereotypical suburb. Everyone who lives there pretty much knows everyone else—not necessarily intimately, but by reputation, occupation, and observation. The houses were built at about the same time, and most of them tend to be a similar style and in the same general price range.

There are a few places that stand out, however. There's Jodine's house at the end of the block—the one with the Mercedes and the Cadillac SUV parked in the driveway. Jodine and her husband have built an addition and put in a swimming pool. Then there is Alecia's house, down the street, the one that hasn't been painted in a number of years, where the lawn has a generous sprinkling of dandelions and the car in the driveway is a ten-year-old minivan with a crumpled front fender.

Jodine and Alecia's houses represent the extremes of this particular neighborhood. Jodine and her family, with their Mercedes and their swimming pool, appear to be wealthier than anyone else, but they aren't wealthy enough to move to the gated community north of town. Other families still run into them at the grocery store, work with them in PTA projects, eat in the same restaurants, and get together with them at neighborhood barbecues. Alecia, in the neglected house and driving the old minivan, appears to be poorer than anyone else, but she isn't poor enough to have to move to a less expensive community. Her family might get some of their clothes at the wealthier families' garage sales, but their children still go to the same schools and play together, and they still socialize with their neighbors. Alecia and Jodine might not be the best of friends, but they know each other and have overlapping circles of friends and acquaintances.

YOUR FINANCIAL NEIGHBORHOOD

Just as each of us lives in a physical neighborhood, each of us also inhabits a particular "financial neighborhood." On the high end are what appear to be the wealthiest people we know. On the low end are what we assume to be the poorest people we know. Of course, since talking about one's income and financial net worth is such a taboo in our society, we don't really know how rich or poor other people are. We judge them to be higher or lower than ourselves based on what we can see of their lifestyles: the houses they live in, the cars they drive, the clothes they wear, whether they have someone come in to clean their houses or do it themselves, what they talk about, their education, their jobs, and whether their family vacations tend to be camping trips or Mediterranean cruises.

Within a given financial neighborhood, there is a significant overlap of certain attitudes, beliefs, and definitions about money, such as the following:

- The definition of what it means to be financially rich and poor
- The relative importance and priority of saving, investing, budgeting, and planning for the future
- Charitable giving
- One's financial duty to others: family, friends, neighbors, strangers
- Financial priorities: what is more important and what is less important
- What it means to be financially responsible
- How money works: earning, spending, saving, borrowing
- The appropriate financial roles for parents, siblings, children, grandparents, neighbors, church members, and citizens
- Debt
- Estate planning
- Financially giving to or sharing with friends and family members who are less well off or in a financial crisis
- The relationship between money and government
- The relationship between money and religion
- The relationship between money and happiness

Obviously, a financial neighborhood will include many individual differences and various beliefs based on each person's specific circumstances. Overall, however, its occupants will tend to have similar money scripts, and their lives will reflect similar financial behaviors. The high and low boundaries of your particular financial neighborhood are anchored by your money scripts. The neighborhood represents a *financial comfort zone* where you generally know what to expect, where you fit in, and how you should behave.

FINANCIAL COMFORT ZONES

Figure 3.1 shows the range of financial possibility, from bare subsistence to extravagant wealth. Obviously, the actual range would be immense. The top line represents the upper limit of financial resources for anyone in the world. The bottom line represents the lower limit of financial resources, the least that someone could have and still meet basic survival needs.

Within this enormous range of possibility, however, our money scripts create self-imposed, artificial bands or zones of financial comfort. These are represented by the dotted lines in Figure 3.2. Your answers to the questions in Chapter 1 can provide a pretty good idea of how wide or narrow your zone would be and whether it would be closer to the upper or lower boundary of the range of possibility.

Figure 3.1 The Range of Financial Possibility

Figure 3.2 Comfort Zones within the Range of Possibility

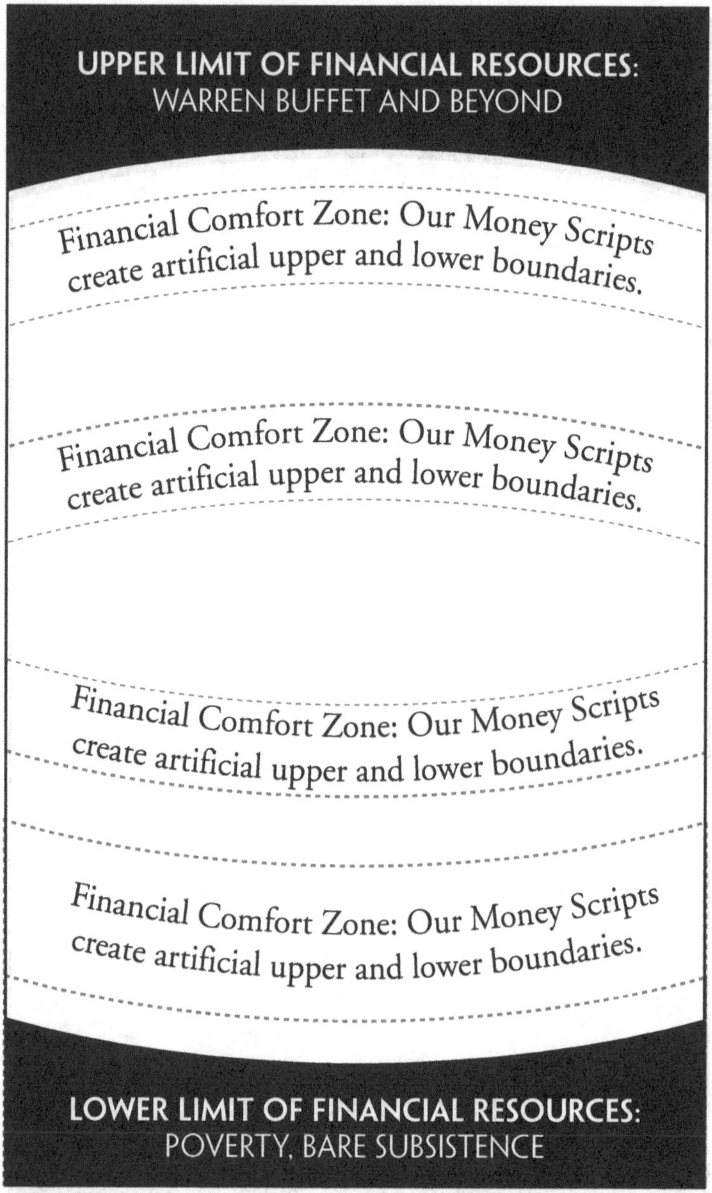

UPPER LIMIT OF FINANCIAL RESOURCES:
WARREN BUFFET AND BEYOND

Financial Comfort Zone: Our Money Scripts create artificial upper and lower boundaries.

Financial Comfort Zone: Our Money Scripts create artificial upper and lower boundaries.

Financial Comfort Zone: Our Money Scripts create artificial upper and lower boundaries.

Financial Comfort Zone: Our Money Scripts create artificial upper and lower boundaries.

LOWER LIMIT OF FINANCIAL RESOURCES:
POVERTY, BARE SUBSISTENCE

How Much Is in Your Wallet?

One way to consider your own financial comfort zone in concrete terms is to think about how much cash you routinely carry. Harry, for example, always has to have $2,000 in cash in his wallet. More than that makes him nervous; less makes him anxious. Lane, on the other hand, doesn't carry much cash, but he won't leave the house without a quarter in his pocket.

Liz, a young mom and then a single parent on a limited budget, never used to carry much cash. She made all her purchases by check and tracked her spending carefully. Twenty dollars in her wallet felt like a lot of money. After she remarried and she and her husband began to build some financial security, she started to carry a little more cash. Each of them had a personal cash allowance of $30 a week, so that was the amount that felt right to have in her wallet. When they increased the allowances to $50, she kept that much in cash.

A few years later, Liz's husband died suddenly, leaving her a small business worth more than $1 million. As Liz gradually came to terms with her inheritance, she started carrying larger amounts of cash. She still makes most of her purchases by check or debit card and tracks them carefully, but the amount of money that makes up her "cash comfort zone" has increased to $200.

STRAYING FROM YOUR FINANCIAL COMFORT ZONE

Generally, your financial success is going to be limited to the range defined by your financial comfort zone. You will tend not to become much more financially well off than the most financially successful people in your financial neighborhood. After all, there are fundamental principles and behaviors involved with making money and building wealth. If you do not intimately know anyone who has manifested wealth, it is likely to feel out of your grasp.

The same limiting dynamic applies to education. For example, Casey does not feel close to or able to relate to anyone who has graduated from college. He assumes that a college degree is unattainable for someone who looks like him and comes from his type of family and his part of town. This belief, if left unchallenged, will result in Casey failing, by default, to pursue further education. His limited view of what is possible will keep him from seeing and seizing the opportunities all around him.

Conversely, it is likely that you will never be much worse off than the least financially successful members of your comfort zone. Falling below the lowest limit of your comfort zone will inspire you to take action to return to a more comfortable level. This might involve taking on another job, raising the fees you charge for your services, or asking for a promotion.

As you approach either the highest or the lowest self-imposed limits of your financial comfort zone, you experience increasing levels of guilt, shame, and stress that build toward an emotional crescendo. This stress pushes you back toward the safer confines inside the boundaries.

As long as your financial status is compatible with your financial comfort zone, you will feel as if everything is fine, even if that comfort zone limits your potential success. The problems begin when your income level or standard of living significantly increases or decreases.

Stacy and her husband, Jack, both come from blue-collar backgrounds. She is a receptionist; he is an electrician. Like most of their friends and relatives, they get by comfortably enough from month to month but have little financial security or net worth. Stacy routinely buys a lottery ticket every week "just on the off chance." Amazingly, one week her ticket wins her a jackpot of $10 million.

Stacy and Jack have been hurled right through the roof of their financial comfort zone. Overnight, they can both afford to quit their jobs and fulfill all their material desires. Sounds great, right? However, they don't know what they would do if they weren't working. Suddenly they can afford to buy brand new luxury cars and a house in the classiest area in town, but they don't know anyone who drives a luxury car or who lives in that area. Suddenly they can afford to send all three of their children to college, but no one in either of their families has a college degree. The lottery representative advises them to consult a certified public accountant (CPA) and a financial planner, but no one they know has ever gone to a CPA or a financial planner.

Overnight, the concept of managing money has changed from making sure there is enough money in the checkbook to cover the bills to making decisions about what investments belong in their portfolio. Stacy and Jack don't know what to do, and they are not alone. Although it seems like a dream come true, this type of sudden wealth can quickly leave people feeling confused, overwhelmed, and even depressed.

Even more stressful than these aspects of their sudden wealth is the way that Stacy and Jack's families and friends react to it. Several family members, either directly or with jokes or hints, have asked them for money. Stacy's sister hasn't spoken to her since she found out about the winning ticket. Their friends and coworkers say things like "Guess you'll be too good for the likes of us now that you're so rich." Within a couple of days, a few bold friends and family members make direct requests for money: a gift here, a loan there, a once-in-a-lifetime business venture over there. Stacy and Jack don't know how to respond. Do they give money to their friends and family members? If so, how much? How do they decide? If they say no to a request, will it ruin the relationship? If they say yes, will it change the relationship?

Moving out of one's comfort zone doesn't always happen so dramatically, of course. By earning an academic scholarship, Andrew became the first member of his family to go to college. He graduated as an electrical engineer and married Melissa the following year. After working for a large company for several years, he went into business for himself. As his business grew and he achieved greater and greater financial success, he and

Melissa moved further away from their families and childhood friends in terms of their lifestyle, their beliefs, their interests, and their goals for themselves and their children.

With a slower transition than that of Stacy and Jack, Andrew and Melissa had time to gradually expand their knowledge, skills, and techniques for dealing with a change in their financial status. These gradual changes can be less stressful and make people less vulnerable to self-sabotage, for they provide more time to learn, grow, expand one's thinking, and stretch one's financial comfort zone.

Regardless of whether the change happens suddenly or gradually, when your circumstances allow you to come close to or go beyond the top boundary of your financial comfort zone, you will begin to feel anxious. You probably won't even be aware of that anxiety or the reasons for it. After all, more money should be a good thing, right? Why would anyone stress out about having more money? If you do, there must be something wrong with you. It's having less money that should be stressful. However, stress comes not only from having less money but also from the guilt and shame that is felt when you find yourself in an unfamiliar financial place of any sort.

We experience stress any time we face a change in our financial status. Feeling stress about having more money is just as common as feeling stress about having less. If we aren't conscious of what is going on, we will begin to behave in ways that will move us away from that stress and back into our comfort zone. We'll unconsciously do what we have to do to restore our sense of equilibrium and comfort, even when that is to our financial detriment. We'll make automatic money decisions that are designed to reduce our exposure to that uncomfortable top boundary.

After all, moving above that boundary might require a move to a different neighborhood, where we might feel judged, isolated, or misunderstood. So perhaps we decide to invest in a business, build an addition to the house, give away chunks of money, or go on an extended or exotic vacation. Many of us will do almost anything to move ourselves away from that upper limit and back toward the security and familiarity of our financial comfort zone. Since we have no experience in managing that kind of wealth, we may make poor business or investment decisions that result in our losing money.

We will also have an automatic drive to restore our equilibrium if we are approaching the lower limit of our comfort level. Toni and Art both had careers that supported their upper-middle-class lifestyle, until Art lost his job. The loss didn't threaten their survival or even their ability to live comfortably. They could have managed quite well on one income if they had scaled back their lifestyle. Yet such a change would move them out of their financial comfort zone—a possibility that brought tremendous stress and anxiety. Rather than take some time to evaluate what might be best, Art immediately signed on for three part-time jobs to help manage his feelings of distress, even though he was advised to first consult with a career counselor.

This dynamic is also seen with successful business owners whose businesses fail and who, within a few years, have already developed another successful business. Falling outside their financial comfort zone compels them to utilize all their resources to return to their original comfort level. In this way, a wealthy mindset serves as a protective factor, inspiring someone to rise above defeat.

The unconscious reluctance to move out of one's comfort zone may also be a factor for young adults who get into trouble with excessive debt. Moving out into the adult world, in many cases, requires starting at or near the bottom of the career ladder. The income level there might not support the lifestyle with which they have grown up. Those who overspend in an attempt to stay in their comfort zone might find the "comfort" unsustainable and obtained at a heavy cost.

Regardless of whether we move past the top or the bottom of our financial comfort zone, the stress comes from a sense of losing our place. If we move out of this zone, who are we? What will others think of us? What will we think of ourselves? What will others say about us? What would it mean to become like one of those people who exist outside our zone? If we don't take the time to consider these questions, we will be at significant risk for poor financial decisions if we begin to acquire more wealth than we are used to or if we find ourselves in a place of having less than we are accustomed to having.

The money scripts that anchor the upper and lower limits of our financial comfort zones help us to define who we are and to identify ourselves as part of a group. People in a particular zone often don't think very highly of the people below or above them. Part of creating a sense of belonging is to rationalize and justify their own positions by making judgments of people who are outside their zone. "Rich people are selfish." "Poor people are lazy." Like a strictly defined neighborhood or a small town, a financial comfort zone is not a place where being described as "different" is a compliment.

If you want to achieve and succeed at a higher income level, you must first come to terms with what it means to step out of your financial comfort zone. For many, this might involve moving into a new financial neighborhood, at least metaphorically, or learning how to be okay with having more money than those closest to you. If you do not take care to prepare yourself for this transition, you will be at high risk for unconsciously sabotaging your financial success or living beyond your means to maintain your self-perception, comfort level, and relationships.

If you want to feel more comfortable with having less, the same strategy applies. Interact with those who have less. Become a student of how they make their financial situation one of meaning, comfort, and ease.

A FAMILY'S FINANCIAL COMFORT ZONE

Our families are one of the most defining influences in form-ing these artificial financial comfort zones. The psychological power of the pressure to remain inside our families' financial comfort zones cannot be overstated. The family is the primary area of socialization, and human beings are social by nature. On an unconscious and primal level, being excluded from one's family can feel like a threat to life itself. In primitive societies, being kicked out of the group could lead to exposure, starva-tion, and even death. It was that way for all of us at one time in our evolution as human beings. Although such consequences for removal from the family group are not often as severe in our society, the primal, unconscious emotional threat can be expe-rienced as just as intense. Being in a different socioeconomic class from one's family can lead to feelings of estrangement.

Pressure to remain in your family's financial comfort zone can be self-imposed as well as coming from other family mem-bers. We call this the "Uncle Jim syndrome."

Uncle Jim was one of eight children born into a family in southern Illinois who described themselves as simple "poor dirt farmers." When he was a young man, he left the family farm. The rest of the family stayed close to home, working with or on the farm, continuing to follow the family's unspoken "We're just poor hard-working folks" money scripts and financial

behaviors that corresponded to their financial comfort zone of
near poverty.

Moving to California, Uncle Jim used his lessons as a hard
worker to move from construction laborer to successful home
builder and contractor. He became wealthy in the process. He
had broken through the upper barrier of his family-imposed
money scripts and had moved far out of the family's financial
comfort zone. His visits back to Illinois always created quite a
stir.

This is how the other family members would speak of Uncle
Jim:

- "Guess who is too good to drive four days [in the days
  before freeways] to see us, but has to show off and waste
  good money by flying to Illinois?"
- "Guess who rents a car because he's too good to ride in
  one of our cars?"
- "Guess who stays in a motel because he thinks he's too
  good to stay at one of our houses?"
- "Guess who is going to spoil his wife and daughters with
  all this wasteful spending?"
- "Guess who has a house so big it has two bathrooms and
  every one of his three daughters has her own bedroom?"
- "Guess who is too good to give us some of his money?"
- "If he were any kind of a person, he would share his good
  fortune, if not with me, at least with Mom."

When Uncle Jim left his family's financial comfort zone, everyone who remained there talked badly of him behind his back. Had he lived close by, the pressure to conform to the family norms about money would have been strong, perhaps preventing him from achieving his financial success.

This pressure is similar to the situation of crabs that are put into a barrel. Any time a crab tries to climb out, the others grab it and pull it back down into the barrel with the rest of the group. Family members can be almost that direct in trying to pull back anyone who tries to leave the family's financial comfort zone.

One reason the family pressure to conform succeeds so often is that each of us imposes our own corresponding internal pressure to remain in the group. Many people who manage to break through the upper limit of their family's comfort zone engage in unconscious self-defeating behaviors and find themselves, a few years later, pretty much right back where they started. This is especially true when the breakthrough is the result of a sudden financial gain such as an insurance settlement, a large bonus, or a lottery win. Although their financial situation changed, their thinking did not, and thus they changed their money situation to fit their thinking. Stories of "rags to riches to rags" permeate our culture and are favorites of the media, with the underlying message of "What were they thinking?" Good question. The answer is that their thinking didn't change to allow them to expand their financial comfort zone.

Because a financial comfort zone has a lower as well as an upper boundary, families can also become uncomfortable if someone moves downward out of the comfort zone. Tammy, for example, came from a family of successful, well-educated people. Her parents were college professors, her sister became a pediatrician, one brother went to law school, and the other brother earned an engineering degree and then an MBA. One of the family money scripts was, "A good education is the way to become successful."

Instead of going to college, Tammy spent a year in cosmetology school and became a hairdresser. She loved her work, was good at it, and didn't seem to care that she lived in a modest apartment and drove an old car while her siblings owned big houses and luxury cars. Tammy's family members were constantly asking her when she planned to start college and what she intended to pursue as a career. Her mother in particular persisted in regarding Tammy's work as temporary, telling all her friends that Tammy was working as a beautician only as a way to save for college. She also kept introducing her daughter to well-educated and financially successful men, with the idea that if Tammy wouldn't achieve financial wealth through her own career, she might at least marry into it.

The response to someone who moves out of the family financial comfort zone isn't necessarily completely negative. Parents, especially, may be extremely proud of a child who achieves success beyond the family norm. The same may be true for siblings. In addition, family members' reactions to a successful relative will vary according to their own money scripts, their relationship with that person, and their satisfaction with their own lives.

Warren, for example, was the fifth of eight children. His four older siblings, having grown up in a poor farm family during the Great Depression, weren't even able to finish high school. Warren, like his three younger sisters, graduated from high school, but he was the only family member who didn't stop there. He went on to become a dentist, built a lucrative practice, and became both wealthy and renowned in his profession as a result of an innovative appliance he designed. His parents were proud of him, of course, and so were his brothers and sisters. They seemed to regard him more as a role model for their own children than as someone who had turned his back on the family's values.

One factor that might have contributed to his family's acceptance was that Warren didn't flaunt his wealth. He and his wife enjoyed worldwide travel, belonged to their small town's country club, and generally lived well. However, they didn't show up at family reunions in a private jet, wearing designer clothes and dropping celebrity names. Even though Warren was much wealthier than any of his siblings, his lifestyle might have been described as being just past the high end of the family comfort zone rather than far out of that zone.

It's also true that Warren's parents, despite (or perhaps

because of) their own lack of education and financial success, expected their children to be more successful than they themselves had been. None of the other siblings achieved the level of financial success that Warren did, but most of them had comfortable middle-class incomes and lifestyles. One of the family money scripts was "If you work hard, you deserve to get ahead." Warren simply got a lot further ahead financially than any of his brothers and sisters did.

RAISING THE UPPER LIMIT OF YOUR FINANCIAL COMFORT ZONE

Regardless of how or when you established your financial comfort zone, it is entirely artificial and self-imposed, so it can be changed. With practice, you can learn to navigate your relationships and learn the skills you need to raise your financial comfort zone. However, unless you change your money mindsets by identifying and challenging your limiting money scripts, you will limit your potential to acquire and enjoy wealth. By using the tools in this book's later chapters, you can remove the mental barriers between you and wealth and raise the upper limit of your financial comfort zone. You will be able to move the upper limit higher, allowing you to reduce the anxiety and stress that can accompany increased financial success and thus to decrease the likelihood that you will sabotage yourself.

LOWERING THE BOTTOM LIMIT
OF YOUR FINANCIAL COMFORT ZONE

Since one of the goals of this book is to help you achieve more wealth and success, it might seem contradictory to suggest that it could be helpful to become more at ease in a lower financial comfort zone. In fact, few books written about wealth and success would even dare to suggest such a thing, as if the mere idea would spoil your ability to manifest wealth. However, there are times when the willingness to lower the bottom line of your comfort zone is exactly what you need to achieve financial health and even acquire and build wealth. This point was illustrated in our study: people who were raised in wealthy families were significantly more likely than those who were raised in lower-middle-class or working-class families to spend more than they made.

Woody followed his father into the insurance business. After twenty years, he was wealthy and financially successful. He was also miserable. He had always wanted a career in real estate, and he had grown to hate selling insurance. Changing careers would mean a temporary but significant reduction in income while Woody obtained his real estate license and established himself in his new profession. If he hadn't been able to overcome his money script of "Lowering your standard of living means you're a failure," he might have stayed stuck in a career that no longer

satisfied him. By shifting his money script to the belief that
"Sometimes you have to go with less to get what you want,"
Woody was able to do what it took to pursue his life's ambition.
He was able to maintain his course without feeling like a failure
and abandoning it to return to a job he did not like.

If you are trying to overcome a destructive pattern of overspending, you too might need to lower your financial comfort
zone. Gaining control of your finances, overcoming debt, and
becoming able to provide for your future financial security
might well require you to learn to drive cheaper cars, live in a
smaller house, and wear less expensive clothing than you have
been accustomed to doing. The willingness to accept a less afflu-
ent financial comfort zone, at least for a while, could be the wisest long-term investment in yourself that you could ever make.

Adjusting temporarily to a lower financial comfort zone can
also be important for young adults. Mason grew up in a relatively wealthy family; his parents were both successful attor-
neys. He was accustomed to a standard of living that included
new cars, European vacations, expensive dinners, and designer
clothes. When he graduated from college and started his own
career as an accountant, it was important for him to become
comfortable with a lower standard of living if he wanted to
maintain good financial health. Until he had time to build his
career and increase his earning potential, he decided that he
needed to drive a used car, enjoy inexpensive vacations, and get
used to meals at home and clothes off the rack.

If Mason hadn't come to peace with this change in his standard of living and been able to lower the bottom limit of his financial comfort zone, he would have been at risk for excessive spending, unreasonable debt, and possible bankruptcy. Mason was able to do this by consciously changing his thinking so that he was not operating from an automatic desire for a higher standard of living. Clinging to an unrealistically high financial comfort zone could have prevented him from creating the means that allowed him to eventually inhabit that higher zone easily.

By extolling the benefits of lowering the bottom limit of your financial comfort zone, we are not suggesting that if you are poor you should "just accept the fact that you are poor and be thankful for what you do have." This type of self-limiting trance is exactly what this book intends to help you change. We believe that where there is a will, there is definitely a way.

In their book *The Middle-Class Millionaire* (Doubleday, 2008), Russ Prince and Lewis Schiff report that the average millionaire has made 3.1 major career or business mishaps, versus 1.6 mistakes for nonmillionaires. This statistic suggests that one of the differences between those who financially succeed and those who do not is that those who succeeded in building wealth tried again and again and again. They didn't resign themselves to failure. They did not give up. They were absolutely convinced that wealth and financial success were as much their birthright as anyone else's, and they pursued this with the confidence that they would eventually succeed.

They learned the lessons that their failures taught them, thus improving the chances of future success. Nonmillionaires, perhaps because they are not fully convinced that success is theirs for the taking, stop trying much earlier.

When a Recession Lowers the Bottom of Your Comfort Zone

In 2008, real estate prices plummeted, retirement accounts shrank, and jobs were lost. The news pundits warned that we were facing another Great Depression, or even worse. Yet as with all economic crises, whether personal, community, national, or global, there lies an opportunity. While we may have little control over the national economy, we can get honest with ourselves and take control of our personal economy. If we avoid looking at our own behaviors, we lose the opportunity to better ourselves. We doom ourselves to repeating the same mistakes, missing opportunities to improve our financial health, and leaving ourselves excessively vulnerable to the next inevitable market downturn.

The true threat to our financial health lies not in the inevitable ups and downs of the economy, but within us. When money scripts are based on overly optimistic and faulty assumptions, such as "the market will always go up," "don't worry about the future," or "I deserve to have it now," they lead to destructive financial behaviors, such as excessive risk taking, lack of planning, or overspending. Conversely, when our money scripts are overly pessimistic, such as "the market will never recover," or "my future is ruined," it can lead to equally destructive behaviors, such as selling stocks when they are at their lowest.

Rather than reacting out of fear, use economic downturns to your advantage by embracing the opportunity to examine your money scripts and improve your financial life to help position you to make the most of the next inevitable market upturn.

Identifying your money scripts and expanding your financial comfort zone can help you to move toward living with a sense of abundance. Living a lifestyle that you can't afford, however, is not abundance. Believing that you should immediately have a lifestyle that is beyond your current means can, ironically, help to keep you stuck and prevent you from achieving long-term security and lasting wealth. Set your sights high, certainly, but in the meantime, live within your means.

CHANGING YOUR MONEY MINDSET: YOUR FINANCIAL COMFORT ZONE

Spend some time thinking about the financial neighborhood in which you live. Who are the five wealthiest people you know? Who are the five poorest people you know? What is the range of your own financial comfort zone? Are you closer to the top or the bottom of that zone? Would you like to be able to raise its top limit? Do you need to lower the bottom limit before you can achieve wealth? If so, what money scripts can you identify that might support you in doing so?

You have begun to identify your own money scripts and have insight into your financial comfort zone. The next two chapters can help you to better understand how some of your money scripts might be keeping you stuck in a narrow, restrictive, and unsatisfactory financial comfort zone.

CHAPTER FOUR

WHEN MONEY SCRIPTS KEEP YOU POOR

Making financial decisions automatically, based on your unconscious associations and the resulting money scripts, can keep you from achieving wealth, holding on to wealth, or effectively managing your resources. It can prevent you from feeling at peace with your financial situation. In some cases, the result is actual poverty: not having enough money to meet your basic needs for food, clothing, shelter, and health care. For others it means living in a constant state of just getting by. There is enough money for day-to-day needs, but there is also a sense of feeling deprived, with no financial security, cushion for emergencies, or saving for the future. For still others, it involves negligently spending to the point of severe financial consequences.

According to a 2008 survey by the American Psychological Association, 75 percent of Americans identify money as a significant stressor in their lives—and that was before an economic meltdown. Certainly, all of us experience financial difficulties and worries from time to time. In many cases, however, our money scripts can unknowingly keep us stuck in a cycle of self-destructive money behavior. The consequences of this behavior range from minor stress to life-damaging and relationship-destroying chaos and poverty. Some of us have recurring but relatively minor problems and financial stress in some areas. Others suffer from an extreme inability to manage all financial aspects of our lives, with money issues and behaviors severe enough to be described as money disorders. Money disorders can and do include full-fledged addictions, such as compulsive buying and pathological gambling, that are as real and as destructive as addictions to alcohol or drugs.

The first step toward stopping self-destructive money behaviors is to understand the money scripts behind the behaviors. According to Jacob Needleman, a philosopher and the author of *Money and the Meaning of Life,* one of the first components of building good money skills is to examine all the opinions you have about money. In remarks to the Financial Planning Association in 2008, he compared our beliefs about money to an antiques store, where occasionally you do find a priceless treasure but most often it is simply filled with junk. He contends that we need to open the contents of our minds and examine our beliefs about money, asking each one, "How did you get in here?" We would also suggest asking, "Do you belong here?"

This chapter examines some of the money scripts that lead to behaviors that can keep us financially poor. The first section involves behaviors that are associated with overspending: spending more money than one's income level and resources can support. At the extreme, overspending can manifest as a compulsive buying disorder, pathological gambling, poor investment decisions, excessive risk taking, and the urge to squander sudden money. The second section examines behaviors that involve avoiding the acquisition of wealth altogether. This includes subconsciously repelling wealth or taking a more conscious "vow of poverty" by deciding that having money is somehow undesirable.

Both sets of behaviors result in similar financial consequences: excessive debt, bankruptcy, financial stress, and, often, relationship problems.

DECONSTRUCTING THE POOR MIND

In our survey, there were clear associations between certain money scripts and poverty or lack of success. Those who endorsed beliefs 6 through 15 of the money questionnaire in Chapter 1 tended to exhibit a higher number of damaging financial behaviors and had lower incomes and net worth. As such, we will identify these as "poor scripts."

Poor script 1: "Your self-worth equals your net worth." This belief was associated with overspending, compulsive shopping, underemployment, and poor investment decisions.

Poor script 2: "It is okay to keep secrets from your partner around money." This belief was associated with compulsive shopping, financial enabling, and avoiding thinking about one's own finances.

Poor script 3: "More money will make you happier." This belief persists, despite the fact that research shows otherwise. We found it to be associated with compulsive hoarding, workaholism, and financial denial.

Poor script 4: "I do not deserve a lot of money when others have less than I do." This belief was associated with compulsive shopping and allowing others to take advantage of you financially. Both behaviors involve getting rid of wealth instead of building it. The younger generation in our study (ages twenty to fifty) agreed with this statement significantly more than their elders (ages fifty-one to seventy) did.

Poor script 5: "I will never be able to afford the things I really want in life." This belief was associated with excessive spending, compulsive shopping, and avoiding thinking about the reality of one's financial situation. In our study, women were more likely to endorse this belief and exhibit symptoms of compulsive shopping than men were. Perhaps the thinking is "Since I can't ever afford what I want, I might as well just buy what I can when I can," or perhaps it is associated with having less money from the start. In our study, men worked more hours than women did (forty-one to fifty hours per week versus twenty-one to forty hours per week) and had significantly higher incomes (an average of $70,000 to $80,000 for men and $50,000 to $60,000 for women) and significantly higher net worth (an average of $250,000 to $500,000 for men and $100,000 to $250,000 for women).

Poor script 6: "Things would get better if I had more money." This belief was associated with overspending and underemployment. Those ages twenty to forty endorsed this belief much more than those ages fifty to eighty did.

Poor script 7: "If you are good, your financial needs will be taken care of." This belief was associated with compulsive shopping and workaholism.

Poor script 8: "It takes money to make money." The financial planners in our study endorsed this belief significantly less than those in many of the other professions did. Perhaps this was a result of the planners understanding that having money is no guarantee that a person will understand how to wisely invest that money to make more money.

Poor script 9: "If I had to borrow money to get what I want, I would do it." This belief was associated with large credit card debt.

Poor script 10: "You can't trust people around money." This belief was associated with hoarding behaviors. Those ages eighteen to twenty-five endorsed this belief significantly more than those ages fifty-one to seventy did.

OVERSPENDING

Overspending is one of the most common destructive money behaviors. It is fed not only by our individual money scripts but also by societal messages that encourage us to spend more and spend often. Ironically, a common governmental response to a slowing economy (due, in part, to irresponsible financial behaviors) is to urge struggling consumers to get out and spend more money; sometimes the government even gives tax rebates and encourages people to spend them as soon as possible.

If you are an overspender, you probably can never quite manage to stay within your budget. You may use shopping as "retail therapy" when you are stressed. You buy things on impulse without stopping to think about whether you need them or can afford them. In the process, you may have accumulated a level of credit card debt that frightens you when you think about it.

Some of the rationalizations we use to justify buying more than we can afford are the following: "I want it." "I work so hard." "I deserve it." "It makes me feel good." "Everyone else has one." "I had a really bad day." Some of us overspend by borrowing for vehicles or homes that are so expensive we struggle to make the payments. Others overspend on a daily basis by pulling out credit cards to buy clothes, snacks, expensive cups of coffee, gifts, household items, and all sorts of small indulgences.

Most people would scorn the idea of taking out a $3,000 loan to buy a bunch of nonessential items at a discount store. However, many of us do exactly that by going shopping with our credit cards. Obtaining a loan requires filling out an application, justifying your need for the money, and acknowledging that you've been given full information about the cost of the loan and your repayment obligations. However, borrowing money—at much higher interest rates than banks are allowed to charge—by paying with plastic can be done unconsciously, without immediate accountability, and without a second thought. An alarming 25 percent of people in our study admitted to some degree of overspending, and this occurred significantly more often in women and younger adults.

Some of the money scripts we found to be associated with overspending are as follows:

- My self-worth equals my net worth.
- Things would get better if I had more money.
- It is not important to save for a rainy day.
- I deserve money.
- It takes money to make money.
- Giving money to others is something people should do.

You may be an overspender if you can say yes to any of the following statements:

- I have trouble sticking to a budget.
- I avoid even making a budget because I know it will show that I am spending more than I earn.
- I purchase things with money I don't have.
- I carry a balance on my credit cards from month to month.
- I am too broke at the end of the month to save for retirement.
- My spouse or partner complains about my spending or debt.
- I hide my debt or spending from my partner, business partners, or financial advisors.
- I make promises to myself or others about limiting my

spending and/or use of credit cards, but I can't keep those promises.

In addition to spending more money than you can afford, overspending can manifest itself in other ways. These include the urge to squander sudden money, poor investment decisions, excessive risk taking, pathological gambling, and compulsive shopping.

THE URGE TO SQUANDER SUDDEN MONEY

Richard knew that his father had worked hard all his life, but since the two of them never talked about money, Richard had no idea that he would inherit $5 million when his father died. Until that time, Richard made $36,000 a year at his job and spent about $45,000 a year. His credit card debt had grown to $70,000 and his home was mortgaged to the max. When Richard received the news of his inheritance, he was surprised at his own reaction. "Most people would be elated, but I feel depressed," he told his good friends.

Richard didn't know it at the time, but one of his most entrenched money scripts was "You don't deserve money you didn't earn." Richard's initial way of dealing with his inheritance was to deny that the money existed. He would speak of "if" he would get the money rather than "when." He didn't respond to notifications and communications from the executor of the estate, so the money sat in a checking account for two years before he acknowledged its existence.

When he finally did collect the funds (which had diminished in purchasing power in the two years that they sat in a non-interest-paying account), Richard decided first to pay off his credit cards and mortgage. Then he decided to help out those around him who were in financial trouble. He loaned his brother $100,000 to pay off his credit card debt, he financed a lavish wedding for his niece, and he bought a house for an old friend who had just finished drug-dependency treatment. He had heard that real estate was a good investment, so he started buying undeveloped land, borrowing as much for the purchases as he could.

Within five years, Richard had given away or "invested" in land most of the $5 million. Unfortunately and predictably, when the real estate market in his area fell into a severe recession due to the subprime lending problems in 2008, he lost everything. Currently, just a few years after his father's death left Richard wealthy, he has credit card debt of $50,000 and has remortgaged his house to pay off other obligations. His sudden money has become sudden debt.

Sudden money is just that: money that suddenly and perhaps unexpectedly appears in your life. You might think it extremely unlikely that this would ever happen to you. Certainly, the odds of winning a fortune in the lottery are remote. Nevertheless, a sudden money event can happen, more often than you might think. There are many ways that people can and do get a significant amount of money in a hurry: an inheritance, an insurance settlement, the sale of a small business, the offer of a buyout from your employer, or a large bonus at work. Sudden money doesn't necessarily mean becoming an overnight millionaire or multimillionaire. Two or three hundred thousand dollars—not an unrealistic amount for a life insurance policy, a liability claim, or the sale of a home—is certainly enough to represent relative overnight wealth for many of us.

Any amount of instant wealth sounds good, doesn't it? What could be the problem here? Why are we including this as money behavior that can keep you poor?

The first thing that many of us do with a windfall is to unconsciously try to get rid of it as fast as we can. This behavior certainly isn't intentional. Take a minute to think about what you would do if all at once you had a pile of money. Make a brief mental list of the ways you might use it. Almost certainly, one of the items on your list won't be "Spend it all foolishly." Very few of us would deliberately and consciously set out to rid ourselves of a fortune.

Many lottery winners, interviewed by the media right after their unexpected windfalls, find it important to announce, "This money isn't going to change me. I'm still the same person I've always been."

Of course they are. That's the problem. One reason people

don't manage sudden money well is a simple lack of knowledge and experience in dealing with wealth. An even more significant reason, however, goes back to the concept of the financial comfort zone described in Chapter 3. Sudden money is one of the most dramatic ways that you can be thrust outside your financial comfort zone. You're the same person you've always been, but all at once this money has set you apart from your family, your friends, and your familiar environment. It's no wonder that one of your unconscious responses is to try to get back into your original financial comfort zone. As far as your unconscious mind is concerned, the quickest way to return to your comfort zone and release your anxiety is to spend, give away, or otherwise get rid of the money.

In our work with clients, other money scripts we have found that place people at high risk of squandering sudden money include the following:

- I don't deserve to have money.
- Money I haven't earned isn't really mine.
- It's wrong to have more money than others in the family.
- Enjoying an inheritance or insurance settlement is the same as saying that I'm glad someone died.

Susan Bradley, a certified financial planner, the founder of the Sudden Money Institute, and the author of *Sudden Money: Managing a Financial Windfall*, recommends that recipients of sudden money put several months between the receipt of a financial windfall and any financial decisions or spending. During this "decision-free zone," she recommends, they should work with a therapist and a financial advisor to examine their values, gain clarity about their goals, and establish a spending plan, a savings plan, a charitable giving plan, and an investment plan. To avoid squandering their unexpected wealth, sudden-money recipients must engage in a close exploration of their money scripts.

POOR INVESTMENT DECISIONS AND EXCESSIVE RISK TAKING

Alex was a self-employed house painter who was good at his trade and made a comfortable living. Divorced and with no children, he lived frugally and had more than $200,000 in CDs at his bank. For years he had resisted suggestions from the bank and from his sister that he should invest his savings in the stock market. In 2000, as he neared age fifty and became more concerned about providing for retirement, Alex decided it was time to make his money work harder for him. He bought a couple of books on investing in the stock market, did some online research, and finally took the plunge. He invested half his savings in individual stocks—just at a time when the markets were at an all-time high.

All was well for a couple of months, but then his stocks

began to lose value. Alex checked the value of his investments online nearly every day. He grew more and more distressed. He sold some of his stocks and bought others. He experimented with short selling—betting against certain stocks—trying to recoup his losses, but all he did was lose more money. Finally, deciding that he couldn't take the pressure any longer, Alex sold everything. He had lost nearly $100,000, half of his lifetime savings, and he vowed to keep the rest of his savings safely in the bank.

Logic suggests that one aspect of successful investing is to buy more when prices are low and sell more when prices are high. However, without a well-structured investment plan and extreme discipline, most investors do just the opposite. During a bull market—a period when stock prices are high—the news is full of stories about start-up companies creating instant millionaires and people getting rich in the stock market. It's easy to start thinking, "Gee, if only I had bought Microsoft stock ten years ago, I would be rich right now."

At the same time, for many of us, the idea of investing is frightening. Many new investors tiptoe uncertainly around the idea of investing, waiting for just the right time, asking themselves, "Should I or shouldn't I?" until they can't stand it any more. After gaining confidence by seeing those around them make money during a stock market bull run, they finally buy some stock—at just about the time the market is at the top of its cycle and ready to start going down.

During a bear market—when prices fall—it's easy for small investors to panic. Seeing a stock or a mutual fund that you bought at fifty dollars a share go to forty dollars, then thirty dollars, then maybe even fifteen dollars is a tremendously scary thing. All too often, what happens is that we watch the price go down, not wanting to sell because we don't want to feel the pain of realizing a loss. We feel increasingly stupid or ashamed of having made what we perceive to be a mistake, become more and more fearful of losing everything, and finally hit the panic button and sell when the market bottoms out—at exactly the wrong time.

The market starts to go up again, but we are nervous, remembering the pain we felt in losing our money. After a few months or years of the stock market's steady gains, we jump back in—often just before another fall. This pattern repeats itself over and over for the average investor, who buys high and sells low. Benjamin Graham, Warren Buffet's mentor, noted in his classic book *The Intelligent Investor,* (2003): "For indeed, the investor's chief problem—and even his worst enemy—is likely to be himself."

Another way to lose money through poor investment decisions is to take unreasonable risks. This can take the form of trying to time the stock market through day trading or investing in high-risk, "double-your-money" schemes. During the steep dollar and stock market decline of 2008, many small investors started pulling all their money out of the U.S. markets, which once again was while the market and the dollar were hitting their lows.

There are also less obvious ways of taking risks with your money and your financial well-being. You might write checks before the money to cover them is in the bank, thus incurring significant amounts of overdraft fees. You might spend an anticipated bonus or salary increase before you actually receive it, then find yourself in trouble if something happens and that bonus or salary increase doesn't come about, for some unforeseen reason.

There is a huge amount of information on investing available today: books, articles, websites, seminars, and more. More middle-class and lower-income Americans are investors today than ever before. More than 80 percent of all capital gains taxes are paid by people who earn less than $100,000 annually, and 49 percent are paid by people who earn less than $50,000 annually. If you have an IRA, participate in a state retirement plan, put money into a 401(k) plan at work, or have a college savings plan for your children, the chances are that you are investing in the stock market.

Just because more people are investing, however, doesn't mean that they are doing it well. A 2008 study by Financial Engines, a leading provider of investment advice, assessed one million 401(k) portfolios. The study found that 69 percent had inappropriate risk or diversification and that 33 percent didn't contribute enough to receive full matching contributions from their employers.

To further illustrate this point: DALBAR, Inc., studied various returns on a portfolio of stocks from 1984 through 2002. During this nineteen-year time frame, they found that the average do-it-yourself investor, who did not use a financial planner or an investment advisor, earned less than the inflation rate. The average return garnered by such investors was a dismal 2.57 percent per year. The inflation rate was 3.14 percent. During that period, the Standard & Poor's index earned 12.22 percent. Go-it-alone investors earned about $25,000 on every $1 million invested in the stock market. Had they simply put that $1 million into the S&P index and left it alone—the most basic strategy an advisor might have suggested—they would have earned $120,000 a year. That's a loss of $85,000 annually.

Why don't investors make wiser choices?

One reason is that just because the information is out there doesn't mean that the majority of us use it or understand it. For many people, formal education doesn't include information about investing and managing money. They don't necessarily understand the economic terminology used in the media; they have only a vague idea of the difference between bear markets and bull markets, for example. Terms like *diversification, asset allocation, capitalization,* and *rates of return* tend to make the average person's eyes glaze over.

It's easy for many people to think of investing as too hard to learn and more difficult and complicated than it really is. The less one understands it, of course, the more frightening it is. Combine that lack of knowledge with a quite natural fear of losing what one already has, and it's easy to see why so many of us find investing a subject to avoid.

If you want to get past a fear of investing, one of the easier barriers to overcome is lack of knowledge. Take advantage of the many sources of financial and investing advice. There are books, community education classes, and college courses that address investing and finances. Personalized help is available from mutual fund salespeople or fee-for-service financial planners. Some investment advisors also offer a flat hourly consulting fee.

To take full advantage of that information, however, it will also be helpful to look at the limiting money scripts you may have about investing.

In our research, men were more likely to indicate that they had lost substantial amounts of money due to poor investment decisions. This could be due in part to overconfidence, which behavioral finance research has linked to poor investment decisions and worse performance in the stock market, and which is found more often in men. In our survey, people who indicated that they had lost substantial amounts of money through poor investment decisions were more likely to endorse the belief that "My self-worth equals my net worth."

In our work with clients, we found that money scripts associated with poor investment decisions include the following:

• Investing is for people who understand money.
• I'm not smart enough to learn about investing.
• Investing is just for the wealthy.
• Investing is too risky.

These money scripts, when left unchallenged, are likely to result in poor investment decisions or an avoidance of investing altogether. Either extreme is bad for your financial health.

PATHOLOGICAL GAMBLING

Henry, a retired construction worker, had never considered himself a risk taker or a gambler. After the one and only trip he ever made to Las Vegas, he came home and told his friends, "I work too hard for my money to lose it in places like that."

Then a casino opened thirty miles from Henry's small town. He and a few friends occasionally drove over to have dinner at the buffet and put a few quarters into the slot machines. Gradually, for Henry and a couple of others, the occasional evenings became once or twice a week and the few quarters became twenty dollars, thirty dollars, fifty dollars, and more. Within a few months Henry was spending several nights a week at the casino. When his social security check was no longer enough to cover his living expenses and his gambling, he dipped into his meager savings. Less than three years after the casino had first opened, Henry had gambled away all his savings, maxed out his credit card, and pawned his car. He eventually had to appeal to his two sons for help because he was about to be evicted from his apartment.

Pathological gambling is a full-blown clinical addiction. The gambling industry understands the psychology of money as well as, if not better than, anyone else, and it uses that knowledge effectively to keep us risking our money. Its use of tokens, electronic cards, vouchers, and payout slips rather than actual money has been one way to distance gamblers from the pain of losing their money. The environment of a casino—from the physical layout (such as having to walk through gambling stations to move from your room to a restaurant) to the artificial sky, the noise, and the lack of clocks or windows—is carefully designed to reinforce gambling's medicating and compulsive effects. Even people like Henry, who would never have thought of themselves as gamblers, can be vulnerable to this addiction when they have easy and convenient access to gambling.

Like other addictions, pathological gambling can lead to criminal behavior, such as embezzlement. Bernice's story was much like Henry's, except that she was employed as the bookkeeper for a large plumbing company. By the time a routine audit of the company's books uncovered her systematic theft, she had embezzled nearly $75,000.

In our survey, significantly more men than women indicated that they had problems with pathological gambling and were more likely to disagree with the statement that it is important to save for a rainy day. They were also more likely to endorse the money scripts "My self-worth equals my net worth" and "Good people should not care about money."

In our work with clients, we have seen the following money scripts associated with pathological gambling:

- It takes money to make money.
- Security is boring.
- Life is short; live a little.
- Somebody is going to win, and it might as well be me.
- If I just keep trying, my day will come.

If you are at risk for pathological gambling, we highly recommend that you seek professional help and check out the twelve-step recovery program Gamblers Anonymous (www.gamblersanonymous.org). You could be at risk for pathological gambling if any of the following statements are true for you:

- I have been unsuccessful in trying to control, stop, or reduce my gambling.
- I have committed, or seriously considered committing, an illegal act to help fund my gambling.
- I use gambling as a way of making myself feel better or escaping from my problems.
- I lie about my gambling or hide it from those close to me.
- I need to gamble with increasing amounts of money to keep it exciting.

- My gambling interferes with my work, education, or
relationships.

COMPULSIVE SHOPPING

Annie knows better, but she just can't stop shopping. Almost
every day, she buys at least one thing she doesn't need. She has
trouble driving past the mall without running in to buy something. At work, she snatches every opportunity to shop online.
She has credit card debt in the tens of thousands of dollars, and
some of this is on credit cards that her husband doesn't know
about. Annie typically has shopping bags full of items hidden
in her closet and in the trunk of her car, and she tries to hide
her online purchases by having them sent to a friend's house.
She has no need or use for most of the things she buys, and she
ends up returning many of them.

Annie knows that her spending is out of control. She has
broken promise after promise to herself and others to stop
spending. She shops to make herself feel better; she shops to
fill the sense of emptiness she feels inside. It works, but only for
a while. By the time she gets home with her purchases or opens
her packages, Annie feels a flood of guilt, remorse, and self-
loathing. To cope with these feelings, she often begins another
cycle of buying.

Annie is far more than an overspender; she is a compulsive

shopper. This addiction, recognized by the mental health field as "compulsive buying disorder," can involve serious overspending and thousands of dollars of credit card debt. It can also be a problem even for those who can easily afford what they buy. Compulsive shopping usually involves the overspending of money, but it can also involve the overspending of time and energy shopping, even when you don't spend a dime.

Compulsive shoppers shop to relieve stress and cope with emotional pain. They obsess about shopping, experience irresistible impulses to buy, and lose control of their spending. Shopping is like a drug, offering a thrill and a sensation of being high. This sensation is not imaginary; it is the result of a surge of dopamine, which floods their brains when they shop or anticipate the relief of shopping. The aftereffect, however, is an inevitable emotional crash, resulting in low self-esteem and buyer's remorse.

For compulsive shoppers, spending time shopping or buying is an addiction akin to alcoholism or drug dependency, with similar social and emotional consequences. When left untreated, compulsive shopping can lead to excessive debt, financial strain, bankruptcy, relationship problems, divorce, work difficulties, and sometimes illegal actions such as embezzlement or fraud.

In our consumer-oriented culture, compulsive shopping is a relatively common problem. According to Lee Gerdes of Brain State Technologies, 93 percent of all the purchases on the home shopping channels are made by just 3 percent of the viewers. Regardless of the product, it is the same 3 percent who buy. Research shows that from 6 to 10 percent of Americans are compulsive shoppers. These are people who are literally trying to do "retail therapy."

In our survey, 8 percent of the respondents said they either "agree" or "strongly agree" that their spending feels out of control, 6 percent shop to forget about their problems or improve their mood, and 10 percent have tried to reduce their spending but have been unable to do so. Consistent with other research, our study found that women were more likely to exhibit symptoms of compulsive spending. Of all the age groups we examined, people ages eighteen to twenty-five displayed the most symptoms of compulsive spending. People who reported experiencing symptoms of compulsive shopping were more likely to endorse the following money scripts:

- My self-worth equals my net worth.
- I will never be able to afford the things I really want in life.
- It is okay to keep secrets from my partner about money.
- If I am good, my financial needs will be taken care of.

In our work with clients, we found the following additional money scripts to be associated with compulsive shopping:

- When things get tough, the tough go shopping.
- The one who dies with the most toys wins.
- Spending money on someone is how you show love.

If you are at risk for compulsive buying disorder, we urge you to seek professional help, preferably from a therapist who specializes in money disorders. You may be a compulsive shopper if any of the following statements are true for you, and you could be at risk for compulsive buying disorder if several are true:

- My spending feels out of control.
- I obsess about shopping.
- My shopping interferes with my work, social functioning, or relationships.
- I frequently purchase things to make myself feel better.
- I feel guilt or shame after shopping or making purchases.
- I frequently return items because I feel bad about buying them.
- I make promises to myself to reduce my shopping or spending, but I am unable to keep them.
- I keep my shopping or spending secret from friends and family members.
- I feel anxious or panicky if I am unable to shop.

WEALTH AVOIDANCE

A second way that money scripts can keep you poor is by leading you to avoid accumulating wealth in the first place. One common form of avoiding wealth involves taking an unconscious "vow of poverty": deciding that there is virtue in not having money, so therefore you won't ever have any. Another method is repelling wealth: believing that money is bad, so either you never accumulate any or you quickly get rid of any that does come your way. Another form of wealth avoidance is denial, choosing not to have anything to do with making, managing, or handling money.

TAKING A VOW OF POVERTY

The need to belong and be accepted keeps us stuck in our financial comfort zones and is a powerful barrier to financial success. One way to stay safely in your comfort zone is to take an unconscious vow of poverty and honor it by making financial choices that keep you poor.

Karl, for example, grew up in a depressed former mining town where jobs were scarce. His grandfather, father, and uncles all worked underground until the mines closed. With the help of a scholarship, Karl became the first member of his extended family to go to college. After graduating with an engineering degree, he worked for various construction companies in his home state.

Even though he worked hard and made good money, Karl was always broke. He regularly sent money to his parents, paid bills for other family members, and donated large amounts of time and money to help build houses for poor families. In order to maintain his identity as part of his struggling family and his struggling community, Karl kept himself in near poverty. Having money made Karl feel uncomfortable because it pressured him out of his financial comfort zone. He felt virtue and connectedness in being poor, so he made financial choices consistent with this philosophy.

Another common source of a vow of poverty is the belief that "If I am good, my financial needs will be taken care of." Margaret was the child of missionary parents who depended on church donations for their work and the family's subsistence. As an adult, she rejected religious beliefs and became a scientist. Without realizing it, however, she replicated her parents' pattern of reliance on the goodwill of others. She worked as a wildlife researcher, constantly struggling for grants and donations to fund projects to save endangered species. She turned down opportunities to make a better living, even though she would still be working at what she loved, because she feared that "the money would ruin her."

Vows of poverty are common for people who work in the helping professions. For example, in our study we found that compared to financial advisors, social workers and educators were more likely to hold negative views about money and the rich. They may make the unconscious contract with fate that because they take care of others, they will be taken care of in turn. This is taking trust in the benevolence of Providence to an illogical extreme.

In our work with clients, we have found the following additional money scripts behind vows of poverty:

• Good people shouldn't care about money.

- There is virtue in living with less money.
- It is not okay to have more than you need.
- I don't deserve money.
- Having money separates you from people you care about.
- If I am helping others, I will be taken care of.

Ironically, the people who indicated that they avoid accumulating wealth, that they are paid less than they are worth, and that they feel guilty about getting paid for the work they do also endorsed the following statements: "My self-worth equals my net worth" and "Things would get better if I had more money."

This finding is consistent with what we see in clients. Even though they have taken a vow of poverty, many carry some resentment about their financial situation and believe that they would feel better about their lives if they had more money. This is an excellent example of the duality of problem money behaviors, in which one's desires, values, behaviors, and beliefs may be in conflict. When these elements are not aligned, it is very difficult to accumulate wealth.

You may have taken an unconscious vow of poverty if you can say yes to one or more of the following statements:

- I believe that having money would separate me from my peers or my family of origin.
- I believe that having money or working for it consciously would "contaminate" my work.

- I feel guilty about getting paid for the work I do.
- The rates I charge for my services are below average for my area and my profession.
- I feel a need to give significantly of my money or my time in order to justify having enough money.
- I give money to charity, or time and services to the less fortunate, at the expense of providing for my own or my loved ones' retirement security or emergency needs.
- I avoid accumulating money because I believe it is unhealthy, unwholesome, or unjust to be wealthy.

REPELLING WEALTH

Paula's teachers said that she was one of the brightest students ever to graduate from her small high school. She was the oldest of three children, and her mother's meager income as a waitress was the family's primary support. Paula's father, who had lost his job with a large roofing business after a fall that left him disabled, drank up most of his small disability check and blamed "rich SOBs" because his compensation wasn't enough. A full academic scholarship made it possible for Paula to be the first person in her family to attend college. She majored in accounting and graduated with honors.

Paula was encouraged by her professors and could easily have gone on to qualify as a certified public accountant and build a career that would have both suited her exceptional abilities and provided her with financial success. Instead, she took a job, for clerical wages, as a bookkeeper for a small construction firm. The work was so easy for her that she took on additional non-accounting tasks just to keep busy. Before long she was cleaning the office, running supplies to job sites, and providing technical support for the computers.

Five years later, she was spending three-fourths of her work time on tasks any high school student could have done, still earning a minimal wage, and volunteering thirty hours a week to help elderly people with their tax returns and insurance claims. Although her life was busy, she struggled to make ends meet and was being treated for what the doctors said were stress-related medical problems. By not fully using her ability, Paula was keeping herself from becoming one of those "rich SOBs" that her father so despised. She was not honoring herself and her abilities but instead was being faithful to the family money script about financially successful people.

One of the top ten money scripts that we listed in Chapter 2 is simple but incredibly powerful: "Money is bad." If you believe to any degree that money is bad, then it follows that people who have money are bad. If those two conscious or unconscious beliefs are guiding your behavior with money, it's perfectly logical that, like Paula, you aren't going to allow yourself to accumulate any.

The behaviors of people who repel wealth are often similar to the actions of those who have taken unconscious vows of poverty. We may create our own self-imposed glass ceilings in our careers, either not recognizing or actively turning down opportunities for promotions or growth that would take us outside our financial comfort zones. We may stay in jobs for which we are overqualified. We may achieve success in the form of well-paying jobs, then sabotage ourselves to the point that we lose those jobs. We may unconsciously choose not to use our talents to the fullest because underneath we are afraid of the success that might follow.

When we pay attention to media coverage of the antics of a few wealthy celebrities, we reinforce the belief that "money is bad." Seeing the grandchildren of billionaires squander their money and apparently their lives on self-indulgent excess can give the rest of us a sense of superiority about our own modest circumstances. It can help to justify our resentment of the megarich and reassure us that we are better off not having wealth. We miss seeing stories of children and grandchildren of the wealthy who live full, meaningful, fulfilling lives. In part this is because those stories are not publicized as often; in part it is because we are not looking for those examples, for they contradict the script that "Wealth ruins relationships and people."

In our study, 27 percent of the respondents admitted that to some degree they seem to avoid accumulating wealth.

Although we did not find any significant associations between specific beliefs and wealth avoidance, in our work with clients, we have seen the following money scripts that appear to be associated with repelling wealth:

• People become rich by taking advantage of others.

- Rich people are greedy.
- It is hard to be rich and be a good person.
- Most rich people don't deserve their money.
- The rich take their money for granted.
- Money is the root of all evil.
- Money corrupts people.
- Having a lot of money separates you from others.
- Being rich means you no longer fit in with old friends and family.
- You can have love or money, but not both.
- Being wealthy means that you cannot know whether someone loves you or your money.

FINANCIAL DENIAL

When Marty was eleven years old, her financially successful family was hit by a crisis that resulted in her parents' declaring bankruptcy. Her father went into a deep depression and became unable to function for more than a year. Her mother took refuge in alcohol. Marty's older brother, Tim, who was fifteen years old, took over responsibility for the family's finances. Tim told his sister to go to her room and not worry, that everything would be okay. So Marty hid in her room, pretended that nothing bad was happening, and escaped into a fantasy world of her own creation.

More than thirty years later, Tim is still in control of the entire family's financial lives. He rebuilt the family business so successfully that he has made everyone in the family wealthy.

Meanwhile, Marty has been unable to take even the smallest step toward managing her own financial life. The creativity that once was her childhood escape has evolved into a well-written series of fantasy novels, but Marty has never tried to publish her work. Instead, she remains totally dependent on her family for money. All her credit card bills and bank statements go directly to the family business office; she can't even look at them or at anything else remotely related to money.

Marty's way of avoiding wealth is denial: trying not to have anything to do with money. In our study, 23 percent of the respondents admitted that they at least "agree a little" that they try to forget about their financial situation (9 percent indicated that they "agree" or "strongly agree"), and 18 percent at least "agree a little" that they go so far as to avoid opening or looking at their bank statements (8 percent indicated that they "agree" or "strongly agree"). Other forms of avoidance include refusing to learn even the basics of budgeting or managing money, allowing someone else to take full responsibility for paying the household bills, trying not to think about financial matters, and being overly trusting about money matters.

For many of us, our denial may be far less dramatic than Marty's, but it can still cause significant difficulties. It is a form of denial when one spouse pays little or no attention to family finances and the other takes care of everything related to money. If the uninvolved spouse is then widowed, this financial ignorance can add a great deal of unnecessary stress to an already painful situation. In the case of a divorce, the spouse who doesn't know anything about the couple's finances is vulnerable to being manipulated or taken advantage of.

Women can be at particular risk when they live in a state of financial denial. Given the high divorce rates and women's longer life expectancy, most women will need to manage their own finances at some point in their lives. When women leave all financial matters in the hands of their husbands, their ability to effectively manage their financial lives after a divorce or the death of the husband can be significantly compromised.

Those who avoid dealing with money also leave themselves open to being cheated or taken advantage of in business dealings. Their tendency to put undue trust in others leaves them vulnerable to risky investments and get-rich-quick schemes. In addition, their ignorance of money matters can keep them from building financial security through legitimate investments.

Another form of denial about money is based on a belief that paying attention to money is somehow not enlightened or spiritual. "I choose to focus on higher things; my needs will be taken care of." This attitude is common in people who use denial as a way to avoid dealing with difficult money issues. They try to bypass the sometimes painful therapeutic work that healing such issues requires. Their pretense that money doesn't matter is an attempt to live in a false sense of peace and serenity, even if their financial lives crash around them.

In our survey, people who reported that they avoid thinking

about money, that they try to forget about their financial situation, and that they avoid opening or looking at their bank statements also endorsed the following scripts:

- I will never be able to afford the things I really want in life.
- It is okay to keep secrets from your partner about money.
- More money will make me happier.

In our work with clients, we have found the following money scripts to be associated with financial denial and avoidance:

- I can trust everyone to be honest about money.
- The money will always be there.
- I'm not capable of handling money.
- Women don't need to (or can't) manage money.
- Those who worry about money don't understand what is really important in life.

CHANGING YOUR MONEY MINDSET: MONEY SCRIPTS THAT MAY BE KEEPING YOU POOR

As you read this chapter, what money scripts did you identify that may be keeping you poor? If you recognized yourself in any of the money scripts and behaviors described here, it will help you to explore those areas further. These unconscious beliefs are powerful blocks to success and can play a significant role in keeping you from realizing your potential. Rewiring the money scripts that keep you poor is a powerful way to open yourself to greater financial success and abundance. If insight into your money scripts is not enough for you to change your financial behaviors, it might be useful to seek help from a financial-counseling professional.

CHAPTER FIVE

WHEN MONEY SCRIPTS KEEP YOU POOR IN SPIRIT

*E*ven *if you have ample* earnings and financial wealth, money scripts can keep you poor in spirit. We work with many people who by most standards would be considered financially comfortable. Some of them are very wealthy. Yet because they are trapped by their money scripts, they live in constant stress about money. Some are fearful of losing what they have, some are obsessed with accumulating more, and some are filled with shame about having more than they think they need. Some struggle with all these concerns. Many are suspicious of relationships because they can never be sure of being liked for themselves instead of their money. Though not poor in money, they are poor in spirit.

Living in this way is not literal, external poverty, but it is a form of internal poverty. Not only can money scripts keep people from enjoying their resources, they can also keep them from using those resources to benefit others. Even though these people have money, their money scripts keep them from being able to use it. Even though they have resources, they are so consumed with fear and anxiety that they are unable to enjoy them. Perhaps worst of all, their money scripts keep them from feeling connected to themselves, their loved ones, other people, and the world.

UNDERSPENDING

In our nation of overspenders, it might seem odd to see "underspending" described as a self-destructive financial behavior. After all, spending less than you take in is a fundamental principle of financial health. Yet underspending, taken to the extreme, can keep you just as poor as overspending can. Unlike overspenders, those who underspend may have plenty of savings. They keep themselves poor not by spending more than they have but by failing to use and enjoy what they have.

Leonard, a bachelor, has worked for nearly twenty-five years as an assistant manager of a hardware store. He is content with his job, enjoys the opportunities it gives him to help people, and earns a comfortable salary. When he was promoted to his current position, he bought a small house. It was just right for him, except that he hated the carpet in the living room. More than two decades later, he is still living with that carpet. He has never been able to bring himself to spend the money to replace it because, he says, it is "good enough." He takes great pains to keep it clean and nice, protecting the high-traffic areas with carefully cut and placed pieces of cardboard boxes he has recycled from work.

Leonard shops more carefully than he needs to for groceries, buying day-old bread, meat, and milk that are on sale because they are at their expiration dates, and whatever other items are on sale, whether he likes them or not. Not only does he buy things he doesn't like just because they are cheap, Leonard also has trouble getting rid of things he doesn't need. He has boxes in his basement full of empty plastic margarine containers, pieces of used foam, and cardboard boxes that he can't bring himself to throw out.

Leonard would secretly love to have a small sailboat, but he wouldn't ever consider buying one. His hobby is woodworking, but despite his skill, the things he makes are never quite as nice as they could be. Instead of buying quality materials and tools, he scrounges for odd scraps, buys the cheapest wood he can get, and "makes do" with the tools he finds at garage sales. In terms of his physical health, he doesn't spend money on preventive care; he visits his dentist and his doctor only when he has a problem.

Over the years, Leonard has saved nearly $2 million, which he keeps in CDs at several different banks. Because he has been too fearful of risk to invest the money, it has not grown enough to keep pace with inflation, and his net worth is much less than it could be. Of course, the value of his savings is almost irrelevant, because unless something drastic happens, Leonard won't ever use the money, anyway.

Leonard's beliefs about spending, anchored by his anxiety and fear, keep him and others from benefiting from the wealth he has acquired.

The kind of underspending that creates problems is not the

same thing as making a conscious decision to live a modest lifestyle. Choosing to be thrifty is a matter of managing your resources well to make the most of what you have. Underspending, on the other hand, goes beyond thrift or frugality. It could be more accurately described as being stingy or miserly. This stinginess or miserliness might not be directed at others, but only at yourself. It is often based on feelings of fear or anxiety, a sense of guilt or of being undeserving of good fortune, or a compulsive need to be self-sacrificing. It is being unable to use your resources to enhance your own life or the lives of others.

Ebenezer Scrooge, from *A Christmas Carol,* is the iconic example of an underspender. Although he had significant wealth, he lived his life as if he were poor. Charles Dickens wrote, "Darkness is cheap, and Scrooge liked it." Scrooge lived in a sparse, dreary home that he did not heat, ate meager meals, and deprived himself of basic comforts.

In our study, 9 percent of the respondents "agree a little" that they deny themselves basic things even though they can afford them, and men are significantly more likely than women to do so. In our work with clients, we have found the following money scripts to be associated with underspending:

- Money should be saved, not spent.
- You can never have enough financial security.
- It is extravagant to spend money on yourself.
- Money I did not earn (such as an inheritance or an insurance settlement) is not really mine to spend.

Underspending may be a problem for you if any of the following statements are true in your life:

- I avoid spending money on myself or others.
- I have a significant amount of money saved, but I refuse, out of fear, to spend it.
- I routinely do without things that would make my life more comfortable, even if I could easily afford them.
- I routinely avoid participating in activities I would enjoy and could afford because I don't want to spend the money.
- I feel ashamed or guilty about having money.
- It seems as though I never quite have enough (savings, food in the freezer, work supplies) to feel comfortable or secure.
- I deny myself basic dental, visual, or other routine medical care that I can afford.

COMPULSIVE HOARDING

Compulsive hoarding is a disorder that is often associated with underspending. Ironically, it can also be tied to overspending and compulsive spending. In either case, hoarders fill their lives and their living spaces with stuff they can't use or don't need. You may be a compulsive hoarder if you have closets full of clothes that you haven't worn in years, if your pantry is stocked with enough food staples to feed a small army, and if your storage spaces overflow with books you never read, greeting cards, receipts, old school papers, and warranty documents for appliances that died years ago. Hoarders hang on to everything and don't make any distinction between valuable keepsakes and just plain junk.

Just the thought of throwing something away can invoke intense feelings of anxiety or distress in hoarders. Areas of their houses that are intended for living space often become storage space, affecting their ability to even move about easily in their homes. In extreme cases, compulsive hoarders have so much stuff stacked in their houses that their living space is nothing but a narrow path from room to room. In our study, 9 percent of the respondents indicated that they either "agree" or "strongly agree" that they have trouble using their living space because of clutter.

It's also possible, of course, to hoard money. Ebenezer Scrooge is the obvious literary example of this. Even though Scrooge was wealthy, he loathed spending any of his money on anyone, including himself.

Dale, a longtime widower, continued to live in his farmhouse even after he had retired from farming. Eventually it became necessary for him to move into an assisted living center, and his two daughters cleaned out his house and outbuildings to prepare for an auction. The basement shelves held two pickup-truck loads of empty canning jars. Packages of dried-out meat in the freezer included about fifty pounds of liver. Stacks of magazines and junk mail filled every available space in the living room and dining room. A newer television set sat on top of an old, nonworking one. The guest room was full of clothes, including pants that Dale had long since outgrown and unopened packages of socks from a store that had closed twenty years earlier.

Dale's workshop was filled with duplicate screwdrivers, hammers, and sets of socket wrenches. The floor and counters were stacked with scraps of wood and leather that he had saved for years. He had two expensive table saws; when the first one disappeared under all the clutter, instead of cleaning out his workshop, Dale had simply bought a new saw.

Hoarding doesn't necessarily have to be taken to such extremes to cause problems in your life. The patterns of behavior described below are less obvious forms of hoarding.

Tom loves to invite friends over for a meal of his special chili. His secret recipe calls for four cans of tomatoes. While he's at the store, however, he buys six cans. He tells himself, "Well, I might need more, and if I don't use them this time I'll have them for next time." However, the next time he makes chili, he has only two cans of tomatoes, so he goes to the store again and buys six more cans. Tom's stock of canned tomatoes thus accumulates in the pantry, eventually to the point that some of the cans expire or are in danger of exploding. Nevertheless, Tom just can't bring himself to throw them out.

Tom also follows this pattern with hardware items. He will go to the hardware store because he needs some materials to fix a plumbing problem. Since he knows he needs a half-inch coupling joint with a forty-five-degree bend in it, the job should be simple. While he's there, however, he buys an extra one, just in case. Furthermore, to be totally safe, in case he measured wrong, he also gets a three-eighth-inch coupler as well as a three-fourth-inch one.

Tom tells himself that he's just being prepared, saving himself another trip to the store, and that he can always return the ones he doesn't use or keep them for next time. Yet Tom never gets around to returning the extras. Nor does he use them: the next time he needs a coupling, just like the one he needed before, he goes through the whole ritual again. Tom's garage has boxes upon boxes of odd parts, although he couldn't tell you exactly what or where any particular item might be. It's easier to just go get another one.

In our survey, men were more likely than women to exhibit symptoms of hoarding. People who exhibited symptoms of compulsive hoarding were more likely to agree with the following money scripts:

• More money will make me happier.
• You can't trust people about money.
• Most rich people do not deserve their money.
• It is extravagant to spend money on oneself.

If you answer yes to one or more of the following statements, hoarding may be causing difficulties in your life:

- I am unable to throw things away, even if they are of only limited value.
- My living space is cluttered with items I do not use on a regular basis.
- Throwing something away makes me feel as if I'm losing part of myself.
- Possessions provide me with feelings of safety or security.
- I worry that if I put things away, I might lose track of them when I need them.
- I feel strongly emotionally attached to my possessions.
- I am unable to use some of my living space because it's full of stuff.
- I would feel irresponsible if I were to get rid of an item.
- I have storage spaces my family does not know about.
- My need to hold onto possessions embarrasses me, or I feel a need to hide it from others.

WORKAHOLISM

Paul is a devoted husband and father. He would tell you that the most important things in his life are his wife and his children. Paul had grown up hearing his own father tell his mother that he couldn't spend more time with the family because he loved them and wanted to provide the best life possible for them. His way of providing that good life was to work long hours. From his dad's behavior and his mom's acceptance of that behavior, Paul learned that the way a man shows love for his family is by providing for them financially.

If you look carefully and objectively at Paul's life, you will see that work actually appears to be the most important thing to him, for that is where he spends most of his time and that is where most of his friends are. The people at work know Paul better than his family does. Every hobby that Paul has become interested in has eventually transformed itself into another business opportunity. During any free time, he is busy trying to do side jobs to provide a little extra money for the family. He feels very good if he can somehow pay for a vacation by meeting with clients along the way so the vacation doesn't "cost" anything.

Paul's children have learned that the only way to be with their dad is to join him in his work. Even when he does spend time with the family, it is usually organized around some work project. In the spirit of "Boy, won't this be fun for us to do as a family," Paul announces, "Get up, everyone, today is lawn day. Matt, you get to mow; Lisa, you get to rake the garden; and your mom and I will plant bulbs." Paul is ecstatic at those moments. "This is really working well," he will say to himself.

Even when visiting relatives, Paul can't sit still. He finds something that needs to be done (in his opinion) and starts "fixing" things—repairing a dripping faucet, rehanging a loose cupboard door, scanning the computer for viruses—regardless of whether his hosts want his help and brushing aside their requests for him to stop.

It is very important to Paul that when he goes to bed at night, he can say to himself, "I haven't wasted a minute. I have been very productive today. No one can call me lazy."

A common driving force for workaholics is the belief that more money will make them and their families happier. If you carry this money script, you are likely to get stuck on an endless treadmill of working harder and harder to make more and more money to achieve happiness. However, this is a fool's errand. Decades of social science research have demonstrated that once you earn more than $50,000 a year, there is absolutely no correlation between money and happiness. People who earn $50,000 a year are happier than those who earn $15,000 a year, but they are not necessarily any less or any more happy than those who earn $5 million a year.

Devoting your life exclusively to work and monetary success is therefore not a way to achieve happiness. In fact, in many cases the opposite is true. If you sacrifice your relationships, your emotional well-being, and your health by working obsessively, you will lose many of the most important elements of a happy life.

Money, however, is only one aspect of workaholism. If you are a workaholic, the chances are that you feel better about yourself at work than you do in any other part of your life. You probably feel more competent, more in control, and more a part of things at work than anywhere else. Workaholics often have an unconscious belief that they have to be productive in order to have any value, so the more they work, the more valuable they feel. They believe that the best way to be responsible to their loved ones is to work hard and sacrifice themselves to work.

Workaholism is often a family disease, passed down from parent to child. Workaholics use work to cope with feelings of emotional pain and inadequacy, and they often have little time or energy left for their families. The time they do spend with their children is often focused on passing down their perfectionist standards. "Five As and one B? Why didn't you get all As?" The children feel like failures and grow up convinced that they are inadequate, but at the same time they often take on the parent's perfectionism and the belief that they are valuable only if they are productive.

Workaholism, which is common in our success-driven culture, is one of the few addictions that society values and that people are quick to claim. "You think you work a lot? I spent twelve hours at the office yesterday!" Financial rewards, promotions, and praise help to keep workaholics stuck in their belief that "work is the most important thing in life." Although your boss may love your workaholic ways, in the end your boss might be the only one around to love you. Spouses and children will accept only so many nights and weekends at work, missed events, and canceled holidays before they withdraw and get their needs for human connection met in other ways.

The amount of money you earn has nothing to do with whether you are a workaholic. You could be a workaholic as a wealthy CEO of a large corporation, a secretary earning a mediocre salary, an unpaid volunteer in a nonprofit organization, or a stay-at-home parent. The bottom line is that your response to stress, especially financial stress, is to work, just as an alcoholic's solution to stress is to drink.

In our research, men were more likely than women to report working longer hours and exhibiting symptoms of workaholism. Money scripts associated with workaholism include the following:

- If someone asked me how much I earned, I would probably tell them I earn less than I actually do.
- I have to work hard to be sure I have enough money.
- More money will make me happier.
- If I am good, my financial needs will be taken care of.
- People should work for their money and not be given financial handouts.

If you agree with one or more of the statements on the next page, workaholism could be a problem for you. If you agree with several of the statements, we suggest that you take a close look at your work habits and perhaps consult a counselor about the role of work in your life.

- I generally work more than fifty hours a week.
- Even if a job starts out at forty hours a week, I will typically end up working longer hours eventually.
- I feel a need to constantly stay busy.
- I have difficulty relaxing and having fun.
- I have difficulty finishing projects because I feel as if they are never quite perfect enough.
- I can't stop working on a project until it is finished, even if it means missing meals, working hours without taking a break, or canceling fun things that I had planned on doing.
- I avoid starting projects or activities because I am afraid I won't be able to do them perfectly.
- I find it difficult to delegate work to others.
- Family members, employees, or coworkers complain that I am so focused on my to-do lists that I ignore them or brush aside their needs and concerns.
- I consistently miss important family events because I am working.
- Family members complain about how much I work.
- I forget conversations or events because I am so preoccupied with planning and work.
- I feel guilty when I am not working.
- I have difficulty enjoying time off work.

- I react with feelings of fear, confusion, or annoyance to the idea of a week off with nothing to do.
- I have gone twelve months without taking a vacation.
- I check my work e-mail or phone messages more than once a day on my days off.
- I am so overbooked that I sometimes forget appointments.
- While talking to someone on the phone, I also habitually play a computer game, read and even answer e-mail, or busy myself with other tasks.
- I have trouble sleeping because I am thinking about work.
- I am unable or unwilling to say no if I am asked to work extra hours or take on extra projects.
- I have made promises to myself or others about working less, but I have been unable to keep them.

CHANGING YOUR MONEY MINDSET: MONEY SCRIPTS THAT MAY BE KEEPING YOU POOR IN SPIRIT

Did you recognize any of your own beliefs and patterns of behavior in this chapter? If so, what were they? Behaviors such as underspending, hoarding, and workaholism may contribute to apparent financial success. They do not, however, help you to live with a sense of abundance or fulfill your potential for true wealth. Overcoming these limiting money scripts can help you to create a life that is genuinely successful and satisfying because it helps you to attain richness of spirit as well as material comfort and security.

CHAPTER SIX

MONEY SCRIPTS
THAT PROMOTE WEALTH

In our study and in our work with clients, we have found several money scripts that are associated with wealth and achievement. In particular, affirmative answers to the first four items of the questionnaire in Chapter 1 are strongly associated with higher income and net worth. We will call these "wealth scripts." In fact, we were shocked by how strongly the first two beliefs were associated with wealth. If you take nothing else from this book, take these first two wealth scripts with you.

Wealth script 1: It is important to save for a rainy day. We all know that saving is good, right? However, of the seventy-two beliefs included in our survey, the belief that it is important to save for the future explained 75 percent of the difference between those who were wealthy and those who were not. This belief shows how critical to wealth is the old adage "It is not how much you make that is important; it is how much you save." Those in our survey who indicated that they disagreed with this statement were more likely to overspend, have higher credit card debt, and have gambling problems. Those between the ages of thirty-one and seventy endorsed this belief significantly more than those between the ages of eighteen and twenty-one.

Wealth script 2: Giving money to others is something people should do. To be honest, we were surprised that this belief was so strongly associated with wealth. However, it makes sense on a spiritual level. In order to receive, we have to give. Yet this money script has a dark side: this belief is also associated with higher debt. Before you can give money to others, it must be yours first.

Wealth script 3: Money buys freedom. Wealthy people tend to agree with this money script more than those who don't have wealth. Money can indeed offer freedom and increase your available choices, and many of the wealthy experience this firsthand.

Wealth script 4: I have to work hard to be sure I have enough money. There is definitely a correlation between hard work and greater wealth. Working longer hours and believing that hard work is necessary were associated with increased income and net worth. According to Prince and Schiff's *The Middle-Class Millionaire*, the average millionaire works hard, putting in an average of seventy hours a week. Millionaires are five times more likely than their nonmillionaire counterparts to always be available by e-mail, four times more likely to work nights, and three times more likely to be in the office or the store on weekends.

In fact, in our survey, the top earners and individuals with the highest net worth also stated that their family members complained about how much they worked. Workaholism is a potential downside to this wealth script. If those you love complain about the number of hours you work, it is an important signal for you to make some adjustments. Wealth is great, but it can never give you loving relationships. We firmly believe, however, that you don't have to sacrifice family and free time to achieve wealth. You can have both.

Wealth script 5: I deserve money. The belief that you deserve good things in life is critical to your ability to attract and appreciate abundance. However, our survey showed a dark side to this belief: higher levels of credit card debt. It seems that just as the wealthy believe that they have the right to money, so do those with high debt. Our guess is that those with higher credit card debt, while believing they deserve money, may be spending money that is not theirs to spend. In addition, they have probably not endorsed the more important belief associated with wealth: "It is important to save for a rainy day." In our study, women were significantly more likely to endorse this belief, for better or for worse. In the next chapter, we'll explain how beliefs like this can cause problems within the family.

CHAPTER SEVEN

MONEY SCRIPTS: WHAT'S YOUR FAMILY LEGACY?

*M*oney scripts can cause a great deal of stress in relationships, especially within families. Conflicting money issues contribute to painful interactions with parents, spouses, children, and friends. Parents may use money and the promise of an inheritance to manipulate or control their children. Resentments over financial inequalities and inheritances can divide families for generations. Expectations about financial behavior can lock family members into careers they hate, cause stress in their marriages, and drive wedges between family members.

MONEY SCRIPTS ARE GENERATIONAL

Money scripts are passed down from generation to generation, carrying an impact from parents to children to grandchildren. Many of us are unknowingly following money scripts that were originally developed during the lives of our grandparents, great-grandparents, or even earlier ancestors. When we research and carefully examine our family histories, we can see multigenerational financial patterns and beliefs.

During the Great Depression of the 1930s, many people lost their land, their homes, and their businesses. Edgar, however, was luckier than most. He and his father both worked for one of the large gold mines that thrived during that time; Edgar was a young engineer, and his father was a hard-rock miner. A tough, abusive man, Edgar's father taught his son by example that "Being stronger and smarter than the other guy is the way to get ahead." Edgar applied that teaching beyond his job. As area farmers and ranchers lost their land to foreclosure and drought, he bought up every piece of property that he could. He adapted his father's belief to a money script of "Someone else's weakness and misfortune is a strong man's opportunity."

By the time his three sons came home from military service at the end of World War II, Edgar was a wealthy man. He gave each of them a substantial amount of property and told them, "That's all you're going to get; now go make your own way."

Howard, the oldest son, did exactly that, by developing land and building homes for returning GIs. He adapted the family money scripts to the beliefs that "More money equals more respect" and "It doesn't matter how you make your money; having it is what matters." He and his company were respected, but it was a grudging respect, accompanied by persistent rumors that he paid off local officials, used shoddy building material in his houses, and disregarded the safety and well-being of his workers.

Howard's son, Danny, grew up secretly ashamed of his father's reputation, so he rejected Howard's money scripts. Danny went to the opposite extreme, with a belief that "Money is bad, and the people who care about it are selfish." He dropped out of school, joined the Peace Corps, and refused to acknowledge or accept any of the family wealth.

Howard's daughter, Carrie, embraced a revised version of her father's money scripts: "It doesn't matter where your money came from; it's what you do with it that matters." She moved away from her home state, married a man who came from old family wealth, became a patron of charities and the arts, and did her best to ignore the origins of her money.

All three generations in this family unconsciously shaped their lives around adaptations of the family money belief that taking advantage of someone else is the way to build wealth. Their actions with money were not necessarily sensible or logical. Nor could any of them, without exploring the past, have identified the origins of their money behaviors and money scripts and allowed themselves to consider the many other possibilities for creating wealth. Yet all their behaviors, viewed in the context that created the original money script, made perfect sense.

Like Edgar and his children and grandchildren, we either accept our inherited money scripts outright or modify them to cope with different situations. When our adaptations are unconscious or reactionary, however, the modified money scripts are also likely to be imbalanced and will not necessarily be more functional than the original ones.

An extreme reaction in the opposite direction of a certain money script or behavior can be just as problematic. Although the outside result can look totally different, extreme money scripts lead to extreme behaviors, such as the rejection of the family wealth by Howard's son. Another common example would be an overspender with a child who becomes an extreme saver. A daughter who grows up seeing the negative consequences of a parent's spending habits may decide to do things differently. She may create a life for herself of relative deprivation, not allowing even indulgences she could easily afford. Her children, growing up in such deprivation, might well begin another generational cycle of overspending. Thus, the pattern of unexamined money scripts and extreme behaviors would continue.

FINANCIAL ENABLING

How do you say no to your children about money—especially if it is for something they think they "need"? In too many cases, the answer is "We don't." An inability to say no to gifts or monetary requests can be a big problem for both the giver and the receiver.

Helping children and other family members financially isn't necessarily the wrong thing to do. At times, however, help becomes enabling. *Financial enabling* is financial help that allows others to avoid responsibility for their lives or for the consequences of their financial behaviors. It involves providing for others financially what they should be able to provide for themselves. Financial enabling is short-term help that hurts in the long run. Ultimately, bailing someone out isn't likely to help them.

Scott, a retired executive who had ample financial security, called his financial planner and asked to have $20,000 transferred from his investment portfolio. He wanted the check sent to the planner's office instead of mailed to his home or deposited directly into his bank account because, he explained a bit sheepishly, he didn't want his wife to know about the withdrawal. "I have to buy my daughter a new car. She totaled hers over the weekend, and she doesn't want her mother to know about it." This was his daughter's third alcohol-related accident and the fourth time he had bought her a new car. "I know I probably shouldn't do this," Scott said. "But how can I refuse to help her when I have so much?"

Financial enabling is not limited to parents who have plenty of money. Harold, a custodian, and his wife, Patsy, a waitress, were determined that their children would have the education and advantages that they had not had. They worked extra hours to send their two sons to summer camp, give them music lessons, and buy them cars. They refinanced their house to help pay college tuition. Even after the boys grew up, Patsy and Harold helped them out every time they got into financial trouble—so, of course, the boys kept making irresponsible financial decisions and kept coming back to Mom and Dad for more money. Instead of enjoying retirement, Harold and Patsy were still working well into their seventies, not because they wanted to but because they had spent so much money helping their children that they had little left for themselves.

Harold and Patsy's behavior is an example of one of the more common types of financial enabling: parents who pay for their children's college education when their own retirement is insufficiently funded. Ironically, this sacrifice can turn out to be costly for the children as well as the parents. Some advisors are currently suggesting that a child will spend much more money—in some cases, five to ten times more—supporting elderly parents who didn't fund their retirement than the child would have spent for a college education. This burden may very well happen at a time in the child's adult life when his or her own family is experiencing its greatest financial challenges.

Financial enabling typically grows out of genuine care and concern. It can also be driven by guilt over mistakes that the parents made in the past. When the parents realize that their giving has led to their children growing up to be self-centered or financially irresponsible, the most common reaction is not to stop the excessive giving; instead, feeling guilty and at fault for having created the situation, the parents respond by continuing to give. This only perpetuates the problem and increases the chances that their children will eventually experience a very painful awakening when they finally have to take care of themselves.

Financial enabling often seems to bring family members closer together, but it can also create many more problems than it solves. These include the following:

- Resentment and anger on the part of the enablers and other family members
- A sense of entitlement, often mixed with resentment, on the part of the recipients
- Unspoken, perhaps even unconscious, expectations or pressure on the part of the enablers for certain behavior in return for the financial help (such as "If I give you the down payment on a house, you'll continue to live close to home")
- A lack of motivation, passion, innovation, creativity, and drive on the part of the recipients
- Mutual frustration that can damage relationships
- A shocking realization for the recipients, once the enabler's financial support stops, of the consequences of having lived their lives as financial infants

Although financial enabling occurs most often between family members, especially parents and children, it can also develop in other relationships. You may have a friend, for example, who borrows small sums and neglects to pay them back or who never seems to take a turn picking up the restaurant tab. Professionals who charge fees for their services can enable clients by allowing them to cancel appointments at the last minute for any reason without any financial consequences. Tolerating such behaviors can enable other people to be financially irresponsible.

Denise and Cara formed a business partnership and took out

a loan to remodel a building and open a travel agency. Without asking her partner, Denise spent several thousand dollars of the loan proceeds on an elaborate antique mirror and coat-rack for the waiting area. Cara was furious, because she thought the expense was too extravagant for their fledgling business and because of Denise's lack of courtesy in not consulting her. Nevertheless, not wanting to get into an argument, she didn't challenge Denise's purchase. Cara's enabling of her partner's unwise use of their joint funds helped to establish a destructive pattern of financial mismanagement that eventually caused the business to fail and led to the destruction of the friendship.

In our study, those who "agree" or "strongly agree" that they give money to others even though they can't afford it (10 percent), sacrifice their financial well-being for the sake of others (7 percent), and have trouble saying no to requests for money (12 percent) were more likely to agree that "It is okay to keep secrets from my partner about money" and "I do not deserve a lot of money when others have less than I do." They also indicated that they disagreed that "There will always be enough money for the things I want."

In our work with clients, we also see the following money scripts related to financial enabling:

- If you take care of your children now, they'll take care of you later.
- Giving money equals giving love.

- If you have more than enough, it's your duty to take care of less fortunate family members.
- If you hold others financially responsible, they will reject you.
- One of the ways to keep friends and family close is to give them gifts and loan them money.

If any of the following statements apply to you, you may be a financial enabler:

- I give money to others even though I can't afford it.
- I have trouble saying no to requests for money from my children, friends, or family members.
- I sacrifice my own financial well-being for the sake of family, friends, charitable causes, or clients.
- I give or lend money without discussing and making clear arrangements for its repayment.
- I feel resentment and anger after I have given money to others.
- I feel taken advantage of or as if I am being regarded as "the bank."
- I lend money and keep it a secret or hide the exact nature of the transaction from my spouse, significant other, or other family members.
- After loaning money to others, I have trouble holding them accountable if they fail to live up to the loan agreement.

FINANCIAL DEPENDENCY

The counterpart to financial enabling is financial dependency. A common form this takes is adult children who rely on their parents for financial support, but it can take many other forms as well.

Nicole's great-grandfather built a small tailor shop into a successful chain of department stores—helped along the way, according to family stories, by making a fortune in bootlegging during Prohibition. Nicole, like all of her cousins, gets a sizable check every month from her trust fund. Ashamed of having so much money and of the source of the family wealth, she is constantly searching for a career that will allow her to feel useful, competent, and self-fulfilled.

At thirty-six years old, Nicole is still searching. Not needing to earn an income from any of her professional endeavors, she has taught kindergarten in an inner-city school, backpacked across Europe, worked on an organic farm, volunteered in a nonprofit environmental organization, and earned three undergraduate and two masters' degrees. She is currently taking a welding class so she can create scrap-metal sculpture. Never able to fully commit, she has moved from one intimate relationship to another. Nicole has little incentive to weather any tough times in either a job or a relationship. She cuts and runs when things get uncomfortable, missing opportunity after opportunity to learn and grow.

Corrine's parents divorced when she was ten. Her adult life went from one crisis to another. Every few years she would get herself into a significant financial crisis, which would require her father to bail her out. She would "announce" these moments by checking herself into a hospital for depression or a nervous breakdown. Dad would arrive, and she would tearfully share her latest dilemma. Dad would then dutifully use all his financial and professional resources to dig her out of her mess. Predictably, over the years each crisis got worse and worse.

The turning point for Dad was the day that Corrine once again entered the hospital for a "depressive episode," then disclosed that she had embezzled $100,000 from her employer in the last four years. Dad immediately called in the best attorneys, wrote a check to cover the employer's loss, and gave Corrine several thousand dollars. Then he told her, "This is the last time. You're not getting another penny from me as long as I live. From now on, you can clean up your own messes."

He had said the same thing in the past yet had never been able to follow through. This time, however, he went to get professional help to keep his commitment. True to form, six months later Corrine came to her dad in yet another financial crisis. This time he was able to stand his ground and say no.

After several years of struggle, Corrine slowly began to take responsibility for her finances. For a long time, she was angry at her dad for "cutting her off" and "not caring," but she and her father eventually reconciled their relationship. In the end, they were both able to see that his financial enabling had served only to prolong her irresponsible behaviors and the resulting financial stress and emotional pain. Although Corrine's father had been trying to help, his behavior had actually kept her from experiencing the full consequences of her actions. Until she was finally forced to face those consequences, she was unmotivated and unable to change.

Financial dependency within families is certainly not limited to children being the dependents and parents the enablers. Milo, a road-construction contractor, started his own business and within a few years was a wealthy man. Once that happened, his widowed mother quit her job and said, "It's your turn to take care of me." Initially, Milo was fine with this. Over the years, however, his mom's demands escalated: she expected bigger and better homes, trips, spas, and cars. One day she called to tell Milo that she wanted the latest model of a BMW convertible. She had last year's model, which he had bought for her, so this time Milo said no. For several years he had been spending more money than he was earning, and he was working with a financial advisor to change his destructive money habits. However, Milo's mother wasn't willing to take no for an answer. She told her son, "I'm not speaking to you until you buy me that car."

She kept her promise and did not speak to him for more than three years. Milo finally bought back the relationship by showing up in her driveway with yet another new car. During that time, Milo had made a great deal of progress toward financial balance in his life, yet he was unable to break the pattern of financial dependency with his mother.

Mary, a watercolor painter, created works that were hugely popular. She also had the skill to market them effectively in her own gallery. Eventually, after her work had made her rich, she married Zach, one of the clerks who worked at her gallery. Because Zach had always wanted to live on a farm, she sold the urban townhouse that she loved and bought a farm. Even though her money paid for it, the farm was in both of their names. Zach quit working at the gallery to become an amateur farmer. Mary gave him a monthly allowance for farm expenses, as well as paying him a salary.

Trouble became apparent when she discovered that Zach had been sneaking money from their savings account. She didn't want to confront him because she didn't want to rub it in that she was the one with the money. She was also afraid that he would leave her, and she was embarrassed to admit to her part in creating a disaster. The marriage continued unhappily for several more years, until Zach finally got tired of farming, got tired of Mary, and left with a younger woman and half of everything. A buildup of resentment on both sides, as well as a fear of addressing their problems, kept this couple stuck in a pattern of financial enabling and dependency that eventually destroyed their marriage.

Financial dependency can be destructive even in cases that

are less obvious than the previous examples. It is a major reason that women stay in abusive relationships. Abusers commonly take control of the family finances, prevent their spouses from working outside the home, and bully them into feeling incompetent and incapable of taking care of themselves. The financial dependency helps to keep the spouse trapped in the abusive situation. Even if a marriage is not abusive, a lack of financial equality or independence in the relationship can be a major source of stress and control.

Another form of financial dependency that is increasingly common in our society involves the "boomerang generation"— young adults who move back in with their parents. On their own for the first time, young people sometimes find that they can't manage the upper-middle-class lifestyle they have been taught to expect. As a result, they move back home, rely on their parents to bail them out of financial difficulties, or supplement their income with parental subsidies.

In our research, 8 percent of the respondents indicated that they "agree" or "strongly agree" that a significant portion of their income is derived from money that they do nothing to earn, and 4 percent "agree" or "strongly agree" that their non-work income seems to stifle their motivation, passion, creativity, and/or drive to succeed. Those who are financially dependent were more likely to disagree with the belief that "I have to work hard to be sure I have enough money." They were more likely to agree with the statement "I will not buy something unless it is new" (such as a car or a house).

Other money scripts that we see in our work with clients who are financially dependent include the following:

- There will always be someone I can turn to for money.
- I'm not competent enough to take care of myself financially.
- I don't need to learn how to manage money.

Financial dependency may be an issue in your life if any of the following statements are true for you:

- A significant portion of my income derives from money (such as a trust fund, compensation payments, or shares in a family-owned business) that I do nothing to earn.
- My first response to a financial crisis is to ask my parents, other family members, or friends for money.
- I believe that the money I receive has strings attached.
- I accept or receive money from family members without discussing and making clear arrangements for its repayment.
- I feel resentment and anger related to money I receive.
- I am afraid I would be incapable of managing without the money I receive from others.
- I have significant fear that I will be cut off from my nonwork income.
- I believe that receiving money from others stifles my motivation, passion, creativity, or drive to achieve.

FINANCIAL INCEST

Financial incest might seem like a strange term. We use it here because one way to define *incest* is the use of one's children to meet one's adult needs or solve one's adult problems. Such an inappropriate relationship can include behavior with money. Until now, financial incest has been a relatively unexplored topic. However, the following examples, all based on true incidents told to us by clients, illustrate how pervasive it can be.

Since Kevin's mother and father were divorced eight months ago, Kevin's mom has used the child support money sent by his dad to buy herself a car and a fur coat, make a down payment on a piece of land, and take an extended trip. Kevin recently asked his mom for money to participate in the school's hockey program. She told him, "Go ask your dad. Tell him if he sends me the money, you can play hockey." When Kevin asked his dad about money for hockey, his father shouted, "Your mom can pay your hockey fees! I give her plenty of money every month—more than the judge said I have to. You know that new car she bought? That was your money. And her new fur coat? That was your money. That trip she just took to see Aunt Carol in California? That was your money." Kevin is nine years old.

When Brooke and Eric, ages twelve and ten, respectively, go

out to eat with their divorced mom, their new stepdad, and his two sons, they are never allowed to order a soft drink or dessert, and they are told that they can have only one item from the menu. Meanwhile, their mom, stepdad, and stepbrothers order whatever they want. When Brooke and Eric complain to their mother, she says, "It's your father's fault—talk to him about it. If he would pay more child support, you could order whatever you wanted, too."

Sid's wife left him after his alcoholism had led to a DUI arrest and the loss of his job. Sid kept drinking and slid deeper into depression and poverty. He managed to pay for a tiny apartment and buy groceries through a series of part-time jobs. The couple's son, Josh, who was twelve years old at the time of the divorce, lived with his mother but saw his father nearly every weekend. Even though he didn't stay overnight with his father, Josh always took along his backpack—filled with groceries filched from his mother's cupboards. He believed that it was his responsibility to help support his father.

Harlan and Adele have been married for nearly thirty years and have never talked about money. Harlan, a workaholic, has always spent long days at the office while Adele managed the household and raised the couple's three children. Over the years, Adele fell into the habit of relying on her son for financial advice. Beginning when he was twelve or thirteen years old, Luke helped her to plan the family budget and make decisions about home repairs. Luke helped his mother to figure out ways to keep his father from knowing about expenses such as extravagant prom dresses for his two younger sisters. Now, as an adult, Luke is still his mother's financial confidant.

In these examples, the parents are violating healthy and appropriate boundaries with their children, to the children's detriment. The divorced parents are achieving emotional catharsis by discharging their anger and frustration about their ex-spouses to their children. In turn, the children feel bad about themselves. Even if they connect more with the complaining parent, they cannot emotionally distance themselves from their connection to and love for the other parent. In addition, the children may know that they carry some of the same characteristics as the parent being blamed, which may lead them to wonder whether they too are bad. Since this violation of boundaries within the family involves financial matters and ends up hurting the child, this is what we mean by financial incest.

The taboo on talking about money is the source of much shame and tension about money. Financial incest, however, is one situation where talking about money is part of the problem.

Financial incest occurs when adults, as a result of their own fears, stress, lack of relationship skills, lack of appropriate support, and destructive money scripts, inappropriately involve children in adult financial matters and decisions. This can take the form of giving children too much information about financial worries, telling children to lie to or put off creditors, or expecting children to take care of financial matters that should be adult responsibilities, such as balancing the family checkbook.

Financial incest also occurs when one parent shares financial information or responsibility with a child instead of a spouse. This can occur with either a minor or an adult child. If a husband and wife are unable to become financial partners, one of them may form an inappropriate partnership with a child regarding money. Even an act as simple as Will's dad slipping him an extra fifty dollars with instructions not to let his mom know about it is a form of financial incest. One parent is asking a child to keep a financial secret from the other parent.

Telling children the truth about financial difficulties is not necessarily financial incest. On the contrary, when done appropriately, it can be a sign of financial health. If the family is facing a financial crisis, it is important to be truthful with the children about the realities of the situation. If Dad has lost his job and there's no money for anything but necessities, explaining this truth to the children can help them to understand what's going on and can enlist their help in managing frugally until the crisis is resolved. At the same time, however, children need to be reassured that even though things are tight right now, Mom and Dad are handling it. The parents' job is to take care of the family, not to find emotional relief by passing on their fear and anxiety to their children.

Divorce can make families particularly vulnerable to financial incest. Parents may use children as go-betweens in disputes over money, especially related to child support, or they may direct their anger over money issues toward the children instead of the ex-spouse. A single parent, feeling overwhelmed, might inappropriately discuss financial worries with the children or ask them to help make financial decisions. New spouses sometimes resent supporting stepchildren, and remarried parents may collude with their children to keep financial secrets from the stepparents.

For children, financial incest can be confusing. On the one hand, being confided in by an adult on adult matters can make children feel unique, special, important, and close to the adult. However, since they do not have the knowledge or coping skills to resolve the financial situation or provide emotional comfort and relief to the adult, they invariably end up feeling inadequate and incompetent.

Financial incest also thrusts children into the realm of adult worries before they are ready to deal with them. This can result in lasting feelings of fear, anxiety, and mistrust. In our study, 11 percent of the respondents indicated that they at least "agree a little" that they talk to their minor children about their financial stress, with 5 percent reporting that they at least "agree a little" that they feel better after doing so. Since we did not ask the respondents whether they have any children, some of them might not, so we suspect that this percentage would actually be much higher if we had sampled only parents.

In our work with clients, we have found that the money

scripts that can lead to financial incest include "I can't handle money troubles by myself" and "Somebody else has to take care of the money, because I don't know how."

Financial incest may be an issue for you if any of the following statements apply in your life:

- My children take an active role in addressing my financial concerns.
- I feel a sense of relief after talking to my child or children about the details of my financial situation.
- I ask my child or children to pass messages about financial issues between adults.
- I share financial information with my child or children, but I keep that same information secret from my spouse.

IDENTIFYING YOUR FAMILY MONEY SCRIPTS

Tracing your family money scripts can be a fascinating exercise that provides profound insights into your own money beliefs and money anxieties. It can also help you to make sense of some of the money behavior you have seen in yourself and in other members of your family. One way to begin uncovering generational money scripts is to interview your parents and other family members about their childhood circumstances and experiences with money. There's no need to discuss money scripts specifically if that would feel uncomfortable; just give people a chance to tell you family stories that could shed light on what people believed about money. If anyone in the family has done some genealogical research, those findings could also be a useful source for money-related information.

Once you have collected whatever family stories you can find, it might be helpful to put together your "family money tree" by completing the exercise below.

FAMILY MONEY TREE

The purpose of this exercise is to help you identify multi-generational financial patterns that may be the source of some of your money scripts.

On a large piece of paper, diagram your family tree. Start with a box or a line with your name at the center, bottom, or top of the page. Then add your parents, grandparents, and great-grandparents, going back as far as you can. Also include your siblings and your parents' siblings (including stepsiblings), your cousins, and any other relatives. You may find it easier to do your mother's and your father's families on separate pages.

If you prefer, you can use a computer for this exercise. Many graphics programs have tools that will help you to create a family-tree diagram. The important thing is to create a chart or diagram that makes sense to you and that you can easily follow.

For each member of your family tree, write a brief description of whatever you know or can reasonably assume about that person's financial circumstances and behaviors. Here are some examples:

Maternal great-grandmother: immigrated from Sweden alone as a young woman, homesteaded with her husband, widowed in her forties, ran a farm with her sons, and kept tight control of the purse strings and decisions even after her children were grown.

Maternal grandmother: divorced her alcoholic and chronically unemployed husband, moved back to the family farm during the 1930s with two little children, worked hard but was financially dependent on her mother until she was in her fifties and her mother died, then she and her remaining brother inherited the farm and ran it as partners.

Mother: got a small amount of cash after her brother inherited the family farm, used it for her children's college education, worked as an unpaid bookkeeper in her husband's law practice but called herself "just a housewife," managed the family finances, was good at stretching dollars to provide for her children even in the early years when there was little money, and later gave generously to her children but remained reluctant to spend money on herself.

Self (female): a saver, self-sacrificing, a financial "soft

touch" for the children; started a landscaping business with my husband on a shoestring, and even though we both worked hard, he says we wouldn't have become successful without my thrift and good management.

When you have filled in the family money tree as completely as you can, go through it and look for possible patterns of money beliefs and behaviors. Write down any money scripts that you may have developed as part of those family patterns.

In the sample above, for example, the subject might have developed family money scripts such as the following:

- Women should manage the family finances.
- Don't depend on men to take care of you financially.
- Hard work and thrift will make you successful.
- Mothers are supposed to be self-sacrificing and not want things for themselves.

CHANGING YOUR MONEY MINDSET: YOUR FAMILY MONEY SCRIPTS

What patterns of money beliefs and behaviors affected your family? Damaging money scripts can create patterns of unhealthy financial behavior that are passed on from generation to generation. These patterns are part of a legacy of financial pain and stress. Once you identify such a pattern in your family, however, you have the opportunity to change it and create a more balanced relationship with money for yourself. By doing so, you can change a long-established pattern and create a healthier money legacy for your own children and grandchildren.

———— ❧ ————

CHAPTER EIGHT

FINANCIAL REHAB: REWIRING YOUR MONEY SCRIPTS— THE FIVE-STEP PROCESS

Identifying your money scripts and understanding where they come from are essential steps toward expanding your financial comfort zone and creating a more balanced financial life. As you have read the previous chapters, you may have experienced several "Aha!" moments about some of your money scripts. Sometimes that moment of awareness goes something like this: "Wow, I never knew I was operating on those assumptions. Now I understand where they came from, but organizing my financial life around them makes absolutely no sense, given my current circumstances. I need to change my thinking."

With this new awareness, you might begin to behave differently with money. For some people and some money scripts, insight is all that is necessary to change significant parts of their financial lives.

Simply recognizing your money scripts, however, might not be enough to enable you to exchange them for more balanced or accurate beliefs. For those money scripts that are more resistant to change, this chapter describes a five-step process to help you change your money mindsets by rewiring the money scripts that are blocking your way to financial health.

We introduced these steps in our earlier book, *The Financial Wisdom of Ebenezer Scrooge: 5 Principles to Transform Your Relationship with Money* (HCI, 2008). There we used Charles Dickens's classic tale *A Christmas Carol* to illustrate how these five steps changed the mindset and the life of the wealthy but miserable Ebenezer Scrooge, and how with the help of modern psychology they can be used to help you transform your own relationship with money. This chapter presents additional tools that we have found to be very effective in moving clients through each of the five steps in order to change their money mindsets and unleash their wealth potential.

The steps are as follows:

1. Face your fear.
2. Visit your past.
3. Understand your present.
4. Envision your future.
5. Transform your life.

Before we can successfully change behaviors that aren't serving us well, three conditions have to be met. First, we must believe that change is necessary. This sounds obvious, but it is not always so apparent to us. Human beings are incredibly tough, strong, and capable. We can continue to labor forward under enormous difficulties and tolerate an amazing level of discomfort before we begin—if we even ever begin—to acknowledge that we really must change our course and do something different in our lives.

The second condition necessary for change is confidence. Even after we realize that we need to change, we still may need to gain some additional knowledge or skills before we can make the change happen. Learning what we might do instead of what we've been doing, how we might begin to make changes, and what resources are available to help us change can build our confidence in our ability to change. Believing that we have the skills to change is critical to making change happen.

The third condition is our willingness to change. Change often requires a great deal of time and effort. It can also temporarily disrupt our lives and make us feel at times as if things are getting worse instead of better. We need to come to a point of being ready and willing to do what it takes to make our lives better.

Following the steps in this chapter will help you to create these three conditions in your own life so that you can successfully modify your money scripts. In each section, we will provide you with one or more exercises to assist you in moving through the steps. We have been using these exercises with clients for years and have witnessed some incredible transformations.

You can learn a great deal from completing these exercises by yourself. Many people, however, find that it adds significant value to the process to do the exercises and then share with others who have also done them. Our most powerful money scripts are difficult to change on our own. We encourage you to consider getting the support of other people who are interested in looking at their own money behaviors.

STEP 1: FACE YOUR FEAR

In asking you to face your fear, we are inviting you to accept the possibility that you have beliefs about money that do not serve you well in all aspects of your life. Given that surveys show that more than one-third of Americans admit they try not to think about their financial realities, this is often easier said than done.

Facing your fear may require a significant shift from not even acknowledging that there is a problem or blaming the problem entirely on external circumstances. Blaming your current financial stress entirely on your parents, your boss, your spouse, falling real estate prices, predatory lending practices, or a particular stock market sector decline may help you to feel better about yourself in the short run, but in the long run it will keep you locked in the role of a powerless victim. It will guarantee that you will find yourself in a similar situation in the future—either through taking irrational action or through fear of taking any action at all. If you believe that you don't have any control over what is happening in your financial life, you may take excessive risks or try to take no risks at all, either of which can be damaging to your financial health.

Ironically, the real power in transforming your life lies in facing your fear of accepting responsibility for your role in your financial mishaps. By accepting your part in creating your money difficulties, you can embrace your power and set the stage for taking control of your financial life. The chances are that you did the best you could with what you knew at the time. Show yourself some compassion for your mistakes, forgive yourself, and move on, but definitely accept your role in your mistakes as your own.

Acknowledging your money scripts and the role they have played, or continue to play, in generating your financial difficulties is the first step in breaking free from the limitations that those scripts have imposed on your financial condition. It is the first step in changing your money mindset and unleashing your wealth potential.

"I KNOW I SHOULD"

Make a list of money-related actions that you have been told you need to change or that you know you should change. Start with three to five items. These should be changes that you just haven't been able to carry out, even though you know that they are important and would be in your best interest. You may feel guilty about not having accomplished these tasks. Examples are making a will, beginning to save or increasing your savings for retirement, paying off debt, buying a more reliable or fuel-efficient car, paying back money you borrowed from a family member or a friend, limiting or eliminating your use of credit cards, and making repairs on your home.

For each item, write down what would have to happen for

you to follow through on these money actions. Ask yourself the
following questions:

- What feelings about the money action in question would
  have to change for you to take action?
- What additional information do you need?
- What help or cooperation from others do you need?
- Would it take a life-altering event to inspire you to make
  the change? If so, what?
- Is this change important enough for you to take the time
  and make the effort that is required?
- How much money would this change cost?
- Is it really worth making the change?
- Who would support you in making the change?
- Who would discourage you from making the change?
- What are the pros and cons of making the change?
- What is the worst-case scenario if you do not make the
  change?
- Can you live with the worst-case scenario?

After answering these questions, prioritize the items for taking action. You might be ready to take action on all the items,
on only one item, or on none at all. Whatever the case, be
gentle with yourself, and don't rush into making changes you
are not ready to make. You will never be successful in making
a change that you are not convinced is important enough for
you to make. Until your list of pros outweighs your list of cons,

either by number or by the importance of your arguments, it is often best to keep your eyes and your heart open to the reality of your current life and just stay right where you are.

CREATE A MONEY MAP

A money map can help you to gain a better understanding of your money scripts and how those scripts have shaped your relationship with money. It is especially helpful for gaining insight into your financial patterns. Through this process, you can gain a deeper understanding of how you have transformed your early associations with money into beliefs that drive your money behaviors. Doing this exercise may generate some strong emotions. We encourage you to stay with those emotions, express them, and write down any significant thoughts or insights that arise. It is helpful, too, if you can share these awarenesses and insights with someone safe, such as a partner, a coach, a therapist, a financial planner, or a trusted friend.

Create a money map in the following way:

1. Think back to the environment or family system that you were in as a child. The exact age isn't important. Just pick a particular moment in time that fits your mental picture of "When I was a kid." If you can, visualize it in your mind's eye. In this exercise, you will draw a chart or a diagram of your family as it was when you were a child.

2. Take a piece of paper at least 8½ by 11 inches, or larger, if possible. Using a square to represent yourself, place

yourself on the paper where you think you fit in your family as a child. The size and position of the square can reflect your perception of the position you held in the system.

3. Using triangles, add the significant males in your family system. Again, the size and position of each triangle can represent the influence and position that each person holds in the environment. Begin with the most significant male, who might be a father figure, and then position other significant males. Identify the figures by putting their initials inside the triangles.

4. Use circles to represent significant females in the system in the same fashion. Again, begin with the most significant female, who might be a mother figure.

5. Represent nonhuman objects or influences by using rectangles. These might include significant pets or influences such as religion, work, mental illness, physical illness, divorce, war, or alcohol and drugs.

6. Represent other influences that were not physically present but whose influence was felt in the environment. These are often referred to as *ghosts*; they can include deaths of people as well as other events from the past. These figures are represented by the appropriate circle, triangle, or rectangle associated with the person or object, but they are drawn with dotted lines.

7. Use the dollar sign ($) to show the relationship that each

character had with money, wealth, or poverty. The symbol can be altered or adapted to represent many different relationships. For example, a large dollar sign might represent a primary influence or attachment, whereas a small dollar sign might represent little attachment. A dollar sign with an X through it might represent poverty, whereas "$$$" might represent wealth. A dollar sign inside a stop sign might represent a relationship in which the individual did not like to talk about money or was secretive about money. Use your imagination in how you represent these relationships.

8. Use arrows to represent the flow of money among the people who are represented in the map. Who gave it to whom? Who brought it into the family? Who lost it or took it out of the family?

Now that you have created your money map, reflect on the following instructions. It is often helpful to write down your answers so you can review them later or share them with a partner, a therapist, a financial planner, a friend, or a coach.

9. Based on the picture you have completed, identify the beliefs or attitudes about money or wealth that you think someone would develop as a result of these experiences.

10. Determine the degree to which these messages were distorted and how these distortions affected the financial health of the individual members and the family system as a whole. Rate them on a scale of 0 to 10, in which 0

equals a total absence of truth and 10 represents total, absolute truth. The more intense the emotions associated with the establishment of a belief are, the more resistant that belief will be to alteration, expansion, or change. For this reason, you may find value in sharing these beliefs with someone else to help determine their validity.

11. Examine the degree to which you have internalized these messages and have acted upon them with little or no conscious awareness throughout your life. List actual behaviors or specific events that represent acting on these beliefs.

12. For each salient belief you have identified, list the emotional, relational, and financial consequences, both positive and negative, that you have experienced as a result.

13. Reflect on painful financial experiences in your life and identify what beliefs or attitudes about money or wealth gleaned from the family system may have affected or contributed to your behaviors and painful experiences.

It is not unusual to have difficulty completing this exercise, especially if you are doing it by yourself. If that is the case, it doesn't mean that the exercise has not been useful or that you have done it "wrong." Save your money map and your notes. You may choose at some point to go back and work more on the exercise, either by yourself or with a financial coach or therapist. At that time you may want to explore these insights further, perhaps focusing on the areas in which you experienced the most difficulty.

STEP 2: VISIT YOUR PAST

Now that you have worked on becoming honest about your current financial reality and identifying your money scripts, you are ready to visit your past to gain more insight into where your money scripts have come from. This exercise takes the acknowledgment of your personal money scripts a step further by examining your past for specific incidents, associations, and emotions that have been significant in shaping these scripts and your relationship with money. This visit to your past may bring up uncomfortable emotions, but it will also provide you with an opportunity to release them. It can help you understand, honor, and gain insight into the context from which your money scripts arose.

YOUR MONEY STORY

Discovering your money scripts is a process of uncovering your money story: the roles that money and your beliefs about it have played in shaping your biography.

Reflecting back on your childhood, write down the highlights of your money story, focusing on your most memorable money experiences. What is your first memory of money or of how it was used? What were your positive money experiences? What were your painful money experiences? These experiences don't have to be ones that an outside observer would regard as significant. Incidents that would have seemed minor to someone else might have been very important for you. The vital thing is to identify the events that stand out the most in your mind.

Next to each experience, write a few words that describe your feelings about what happened: words like *angry, frustrated, sad, embarrassed, happy, excited, joyful, ashamed, hurt, distressed,* or *scared.*

Read through what you have written. Write one or two sentences that summarize the lessons you learned from your experiences with money. Complete one of the following sentences: "The moral of my money story is . . . " or, "Overall, based on my experiences, the lessons I've learned about money and how it works are . . . "

ACKNOWLEDGING YOUR LOSSES

As you recall your money story, portions of it are likely to be emotionally painful. Acknowledging and coming to terms with that pain is an important step toward healing and ensuring that the remaining chapters of your money biography are more satisfying, joyful, and successful. The most stubbornly held money scripts are locked in place by intense emotions. Acknowledging and releasing these emotions will give you the opportunity to look at your financial life in a different way.

It is best to do this exercise when you have privacy and the time to sit with any emotions it may bring up. Write down some of the losses and painful experiences in your adult life. How might those be related to your childhood money scripts? What have your money scripts cost you?

Some examples of losses might be the following:

- A divorce that is caused in part by or that results in financial misunderstanding, financial infidelity, mistrust, or financial stress
- A lack of closeness with your children because of your disordered relationship with work, or the loss of a parent in your own life due to his or her workaholism
- The failure to pursue career opportunities because your money scripts held you back

Allowing yourself to process these painful emotions can be a life-transforming step that enables you to see more clearly and adopt more effective money scripts. Strong emotions can keep destructive money scripts locked in place and resistant to change. Releasing unexpressed emotions from unresolved emotional wounds opens the door to clarity, peace, and new choices.

IDENTIFYING MONEY GRIEVANCES

If you have been wronged or mistreated in ways that relate to money, you may carry feelings of anxiety and mistrust about money, perhaps without even knowing why. One of your default money scripts may be "You can't trust people about money." Like all money scripts, this belief makes total sense, given the experience from which it arose. Unfortunately, when this money script is applied out of context (such as when you are with someone who is trustworthy), it can wreak havoc with your relationships and limit your wealth potential. The insight that is gained by identifying the original context or situation from which a money script arose and then comparing that situation to your current life can lesson the grip of the money script on your life and your behavior.

Think back to a time you felt betrayed around money. Maybe you expected or were promised something and then did not get it. Perhaps you didn't know about something that everyone else took for granted. Maybe you were cheated or lied to about money. Perhaps someone took advantage of your innocence or generosity. Maybe you loaned money or personal property to someone who, despite promises to the contrary, never returned it.

The experience may not be one that would seem large or significant to someone else, or perhaps even to you at this point in your life, but it might still have had a powerful impact on you. It could have left you feeling taken advantage of, ashamed, angry, betrayed, ignored, or wronged. You might have been left with a strong feeling that you need to make things right or settle the score. Maybe you wished that you could explain yourself because you thought you would be understood if only you could make someone listen to you. Perhaps you have said to yourself, "Never again."

Write down what happened and how you felt about it. Then list the lessons you learned from the experience. These lessons might not have been positive ones; perhaps they helped you to cope with the situation when it happened but have not served you well later in your life. They could be decisions you made about how you would act in the future, vows you made never to treat others in a certain way, or merely a determination never to get yourself into another situation like that again.

If you can remember more than one experience of this type, write separately about each one. When you are finished, compare the experiences and look for common patterns. Is this an experience you have found yourself having over and over again?

Next, examine your current life. Are you placing yourself in similar situations with similar people? Are you with safe and trustworthy people but still operating from a place of fear and mistrust? When you are with safe and trustworthy people, are you willing to let go of your exaggerated fear? Are you once again putting yourself at risk in situations and with people and ignoring the warning signs? If so, what changes do you need to make? Are you willing to make those changes? What are you willing to do today?

MONEY EMPOWERMENT

Certainly, not all of our early experiences with money were negative. Many of our money scripts arose from positive experiences with money that left us feeling empowered, joyful, hopeful, or ecstatic. These positive experiences also firmly anchor some of our money scripts, which can then continue to have a significant impact on our lives. We may engage in financial behaviors to try to re-create these intensely positive emotional experiences, sometimes to our detriment. Identifying the times in which money was used in a way that made us feel empowered can be very helpful. It is important to remember that even these positive experiences can cause us to believe in certain financial "truths" that can be just as destructive as our negative experiences.

Ralph remembers his first experience with money. He was sitting quietly as his father and a neighbor were talking. As they finished the conversation, the neighbor reached into his pocket, pulled out a quarter, and said to Ralph, "You sure have been a good boy. Here, take this." A positive experience, right? Well, Ralph's six-year-old mind interpreted the neighbor's action to mean that it is up to other people to determine what you are worth, and you should just be happy with what others give you. His interpretation of that experience limited him for the next fifty years. He found himself in an occupation, public education, in which the understanding is that others determine your value and decide how much you are paid. One can be a great educator, an average one, or even a poor one, but the pay is the same.

When Ralph retired from teaching, he went into his own private consulting business. He found that he was quite uncomfortable quoting a price for his work; he preferred that people tell him how much they were willing to pay for his services. Any suggestion that he might benefit from even the most modest promotion of his services was met with great resistance. He saw such suggestions as shameless self-promotion. For years, he was paid significantly less than others with similar experience and skills. In fact, even his own clients often scolded him for not charging enough. In this case, Ralph's positive childhood money experience ended up damaging his financial potential and the quality of life for his family.

Think back to a time in your life, especially in childhood, where you felt empowered about money. Perhaps you remember learning something about how money works, being praised or rewarded financially, or accomplishing something difficult. Some examples of this might be saving for and buying something you wanted, receiving your first allowance or your first paycheck, winning a prize, or choosing to use a gift of money in whatever way you wanted. Perhaps you cheated or took advantage of someone else and got away with it. This experience might have left you feeling powerful, listened to, competent, or proud.

Write down what happened and how you felt about it. Then

list the lessons you learned from the experience. As in the previous exercise, these lessons won't necessarily be positive ones and may not be serving you well in your life now.

If you can remember more than one experience of this type, write separately about each one. When you are finished, compare the experiences and look for common patterns.

STEP 3: UNDERSTAND YOUR PRESENT

One of the ways in which money scripts keep us stuck is by blocking our ability to take in information that conflicts with our scripts. Blindly following our money scripts means that we react rather than respond to financial challenges; we make financial decisions without conscious thought or awareness of other choices. We behave as if the money scripts are always true, because we unconsciously assume that "that's the way things are." The money scripts can prevent us from believing that change is necessary, from knowing what and how to change, and from being ready and willing to change.

The process of identifying your money scripts, examining where they originated, and acknowledging any unresolved emotions from those experiences opens your eyes to your present circumstances. Once you are no longer tied to money scripts that have lost their usefulness, you have the flexibility you need to respond to current situations with your eyes wide open instead of with reflexive, overly emotional reactions based on your history. It helps you see the present more clearly and become more open to positive change.

REWIRING YOUR MONEY SCRIPTS: GIVING YOURSELF A FINANCIAL HEALTH MAKEOVER

Choose one of your money scripts that you have identified with the help of the previous exercises. Then write down as many variations of this money script as you can think of. It may help to do this exercise in the following three steps:

1. Write down specific ways or circumstances in which the money script is indeed true.

2. Imagine and write down various scenarios or circumstances in which the money script might not always be true. Pay attention to whatever feelings come up for you in this step. If your feelings are intense, it might be a clue that you continue to have some unresolved emotions from a painful experience.

3. Write one or more modified versions of the money script, expanding it beyond its original limited "truth."

As an example, let's use one of the top ten money scripts, "I deserve to spend money."

First, in what ways or under what circumstances might this money script be true or partly true?

• I deserve to spend money to take care of myself and my

family (such as providing housing, food, transportation, medical care, and entertainment).

- I deserve to spend my personal allowance in any way I choose (such as including in the budget a given amount that each person may spend on hobbies, self-care, or individual indulgences).
- I deserve to spend money to invest in my future (such as education, exercise, or career advancement).
- I deserve to spend money on activities and possessions that add meaning and pleasure to my life.

Second, in what ways or under what circumstances might this money script not be true?

- I don't deserve to spend more money than I have (such as using a credit card to buy new clothes that I don't really need).
- I don't deserve to spend money that is designated for some other purpose (such as using the rent money to go on vacation).
- I don't deserve to spend money that isn't legitimately mine (such as "borrowing" a family member's credit card without permission).
- I don't deserve to spend money for short-term gratification that results in painful long-term consequences (such as buying expensive Christmas gifts on a credit card, then depriving myself for months as I struggle to pay off the balance).

Third, what might be some modified versions of this money script?

- I deserve to spend money in ways that provide for my needs and those of my family, that support my goals, and that enhance my life.
- I deserve the self-respect and confidence that come with spending money responsibly and competently.

A HEALTHY MONEY MANTRA

The following seven-step exercise can be used to dislodge specific money scripts that may be keeping you stuck. This process is most useful when you have identified a core money script that keeps tripping you up. It works best when you have insight into where the money script came from, when you realize how it affects your financial and emotional well-being, and when you are committed to changing its impact on your life. Creating a healthy money mantra is a way of consciously changing your thinking whenever you find yourself starting to respond based on a particular money script. Used over time, this process can dramatically change your life.

The seven steps are as follows:

1. Identify the specific situation that is causing a problem, the thought that comes to mind in that situation, and the resulting emotion. We often know that things aren't right because we don't feel good about them. ("I was driving

home from work; I thought I should be working more hours; I began to feel guilty.")

2. Identify the money script that underlies the feeling. This is a very important and critical step because it goes beyond the original thought to the core belief that is driving it. The money script may be harder to identify than the thoughts and feelings in the first step. ("Working harder is the only way to be successful.")

3. Acknowledge the ways in which the money script has been true and did serve you at one time, by noting its original context. Then add "But now . . . " and state how the script no longer applies in your current life. ("When I was working my way through college, trying to get out of the poverty I grew up in, I did have to put in long hours and work hard. But now I earn a good salary, my boss respects me and values my work, and I have the time to spend with my family.")

4. Create a more accurate money script statement based on your current reality, your values, and your goals. Maybe you have already done so in the "rewiring your money scripts" exercise above. It is important to work on this statement to make it positive rather than just a negation of the original money script. Focusing on the negative, even in an attempt to negate a negative, just adds energy to the negative and gives it more power. (Rather than "Working harder is not the only way to be successful," a

more positive and more powerful rewiring would be "True success and happiness come from connection with others.")

5. Identify the value that underlies the new money script. ("My family is the most important thing in my life.")

6. Identify the new, healthy behavior that is based on the new script. In this example, the behavior in response to the original script would be going back to work or taking work home. The revised money script would result in different choices. ("I am going home to spend time with my spouse and children.")

7. Develop a healthy money mantra by linking the fourth, fifth, and sixth steps. In this example, the money mantra would be "True success and happiness come from connection with others. My family is the most important thing in my life. I am going home to spend time with my spouse and children."

Once you have created your healthy money mantra, you have a conscious statement to counter your original unconscious money script. Write it on a card and carry it with you. When thoughts, feelings, or situations trigger this money script, pull out your card and recite your money mantra. Reciting your healthy money mantra can interrupt the automatic emotional and behavioral response to the script. It is a powerful reminder that you have other, healthier choices.

You can actively influence changes in your brain by taking conscious control of your thinking and behavior patterns. Columbia University professor Eric Kandel found that long-term conditioning of the brain can lead to lasting structural changes (*Monitor on Psychology*, September 1985). As brain cells repeatedly send signals in response to a stimulus, their chemistry and shape can permanently change. Therefore, rewiring exercises such as the money mantra can actually *alter the physical structure of your brain*, creating new neuropathways that allow you to change your automatic thinking and habitual behaviors.

MONEY SCRIPTS AND CORE VALUES

Write a brief list of some of your most important core values and the aspects of your life that matter most to you. Some examples might be as follows:

- Living with integrity
- Having a family
- Being a good parent
- Building a business that has a reputation for honorable dealing and quality work
- Mentoring and teaching others
- Making full use of my unique talents
- Giving back to my community
- Leaving a positive legacy

Now write down any areas in which your behaviors are not

in line with your core values. Some examples might be the following:

- Working long hours instead of spending time with my family
- Cutting corners at work in ways that compromise quality
- Waiting for someone else to take care of community problems instead of volunteering to help
- Failing to use talents and skills that are important to me

Look at the money scripts you have identified in the previous exercises. Which money scripts are holding you back from living in full alignment with your core values? What steps are you ready to take today to align your behaviors with your core values?

STEP 4: ENVISION YOUR FUTURE

Once you have looked clearly at both the influences of your past and the reality of your present life, you have paved the way for a more successful and fulfilling future. When you gain perspective on where you have come from, what beliefs are holding you back, and the reality of your current life, your ability to create the life you want will dramatically improve.

TIME'S UP

Imagine that you have just been told that your life is ending. Suddenly you are out of time. You will have no more opportunities, no more possibilities, no more "somedays," and no more second chances.

Quickly, without stopping to censor yourself, overanalyze, or edit your answers, write down a list of unfinished business. This list might include things you would regret doing or not doing, things you wish you had said to your loved ones, risks you wish you had taken, places you would have liked to visit, talents you might have developed, and choices you would have made differently.

This list can give you important insights into the things that are important to you, things to which you will want to devote time, money, and energy in order to build the future you want.

STEP 5: TRANSFORM YOUR LIFE

Step 5 is where the rubber hits the road. Using your list from the "time's up" exercise, think about the changes you are ready to make in the way you live your life. How can you incorporate more of what you want most into your daily life? What goals might you want to work toward achieving? What might you need to change in order for your actions to more closely match your core values?

At first glance, this final step might seem to have little to do with money or with creating abundance and financial balance in your life. Yet this part of the process is the reason that changing your money mindsets is so important. The more deeply you commit to this step, the more of an impact it will have on your life. Like Ebenezer Scrooge, you may find that creating a balanced relationship with money has the power to transform many other aspects of your life. When you rewire your destructive money scripts, you open the way to use money in a healthy, balanced way as a vital tool to help create the rich life you desire and deserve.

REWIRED MONEY MINDSETS: FINANCIAL HEALTH MAKEOVERS

By most standards, Alan had a lot of money: his net worth was $5 million. Yet Alan routinely lay awake at night worrying that the money would someday run out. After reading our book *The Financial Wisdom of Ebenezer Scrooge,* Alan was able to identify that one of his major money scripts was "The money will run out." This script was embedded in his thinking as a young child as he watched his father struggle in his seasonal tourist business.

Every year around February or March, Alan's father would start worrying that his money, which he had prudently saved and put in the bank account at the end of the season the previous October, would run out before the season started again. Although it never did, little Alan had no larger context in which to frame this annual event. For about three months of every year, he secretly lived with the fear that he and his family would run out of food, clothing, and shelter.

It is no wonder that Alan carried this fear into adulthood, even when his net worth had grown well past the point where the fear made any logical sense.

Nevertheless, simply becoming conscious of this money script was not enough to end Alan's nightly bouts of insomnia. He felt a lot of shame around this. Intellectually he knew that he spent well within his means and that his money wouldn't run out, but all the rationalizations he tried did not cure the 2:00 AM worrying sessions.

Alan decided to engage a financial planner who worked in conjunction with a financial therapist to help him with this chronic fear, which was affecting the quality of his life. Working with his financial planner and the therapist, Alan explored the traumatic impact that this scenario had made on his young mind, and he was able to let go of some of the strong emotions that kept his limiting money script locked in place. After a few sessions, Alan was sleeping soundly at night, for the first time in decades.

In Chapter 2 we introduced you to Eliot, whose story illustrates the "Money will give my life meaning" money script. He was an ambitious and intelligent man who transcended his childhood of abuse and poverty and became both famous and wealthy. In his sixties, Eliot realized that his intense drive toward financial success had come at a tremendous cost. He said to us, "I have all the money and fame any one person could want. Yet I don't have any real friends, and my kids hate me. I thought that money would help me find peace and love, but it didn't. I don't have any idea of what I want the most, and even if I did, I wouldn't know where to start to get it."

Eliot sought our help after realizing that his drive toward success had left him without peace, love, or healthy relationships. He worked on financial healing with the same energy and commitment he had brought to his career. It wasn't long before Eliot accepted his share of the responsibility for his distant relationships with his children. For one thing, he accepted that he had been so focused on his work that he had spent little time with them when they were young. After they grew up, he tried to control their behavior and compel them to spend time with him by either giving or withholding money.

With the support of a financial therapist, Eliot stopped using money to control his family. Gradually, his relationships with his children began to change. At a follow-up appointment several months after he had left therapy, Eliot reported with gratitude that the last two family celebrations with his children and grandchildren were the best family times he had ever known. Eliot had rewired his old money script of "Money will give my life meaning," to his and his entire family's benefit.

We also introduced you to Joy, whose story illustrated the "Money is unimportant" money script. Joy kept herself in poverty for years, believing that taking care of her own financial security would be incongruent with her mission of helping others. Eventually, through one of her volunteer projects, she came to know a financial coach. For the first time, she began taking a serious look at her beliefs and behaviors concerning money.

After working with the coach, Joy concluded that keeping herself poor was harming rather than helping her ability to help others. She found a job with an engineering firm, making a commitment to her financial coach that she would keep the job long enough to establish some financial security and take care of herself by getting some long-postponed dental work and medical checkups. She cut back on the time she spent volunteering and focused on one organization that meant the most to her. Several months later, Joy was offered a position with an environmental organization that would enable her to fulfill her goal of helping people in a way that allowed her to use her education and provide for herself financially. She also realized that having some financial security enabled her to donate to charities and help others in ways she had never previously considered.

All these stories illustrate the power of rewiring your money scripts by using the five steps described in this chapter. Alan, Eliot, and Joy were able to transform their lives by breaking their denial and becoming honest about their role in their money-related problems, reviewing their past and examining their money scripts, facing the reality of their present lives and the steps they needed to take, envisioning the future they would like, and then taking action.

CHANGING YOUR MONEY MINDSET:
REWIRING YOUR MONEY SCRIPTS

If you are like most of us, you may have read this chapter without actually taking the time to complete the exercises. It's easy to think that we've gained all the insight we need from just reading through the exercises. If this is true for you, what neuroscience tells us is that you have used only the left side of your brain so far. Although it is the logical, information-processing part of our brain, it actually makes just approximately 20 percent of our behavioral decisions. On the other hand, the right (or emotional) hemisphere of our brain, the part of our brain that is employed when we actually *do* the suggested exercises, makes 80 percent of our behavioral decisions.

The best way to use this material is obviously to engage both sides of the brain: to read the exercises and do them. Stopping at just reading the exercises may limit by 80 percent the likelihood that you will actually make the changes you want to make. If you genuinely want to change your money mindsets and free yourself from beliefs that are blocking your success, actually doing the exercises is important. It's fine to go back and do them later or do them a few at a time. However, please keep in mind that change is a process. Reading about change and thinking about change are important steps toward becoming willing to change, but they often aren't enough. Transforming your life requires action as well as insight. Completing the exercises is a valuable and simple way to begin taking action.

CHAPTER NINE

WHEN MONEY SCRIPTS COLLIDE: COUPLES IN CONFLICT

*U*nderstanding and rewiring your own money scripts is a critical step toward building a healthier relationship with money. Once you have begun to do so, you can also apply this knowledge to your relationships with the most important people in your life. For a couple, understanding each other's money scripts can be a valuable tool for addressing conflicts over money. It offers important insights to help the couple negotiate solutions to those conflicts and work as partners to reduce money-related stress.

While their children were growing up, Eileen drove newer minivans and Sam got by with well-used compact cars. Once the youngest child was out of college, Sam wanted to buy his first-ever new car. With no more tuition payments or orthodontist bills, they could afford it, so Eileen agreed.

At least, she agreed until Sam showed her the car he wanted: a racy two-seater convertible. He was quick to explain that it got incredible gas mileage and wasn't expensive—at least compared to the Porsche, which was his real dream car.

Eileen was appalled. "Are you crazy? That's not a car; it's a cliché! People would laugh and say you were having a midlife crisis. And it doesn't even have room for a bag of groceries."

Sam and Eileen fought for days over the car without being able to resolve their differences. In your opinion, who is right here and who is wrong?

Sara tends to be generous with gifts for her children and grandchildren. At Christmas, the tree almost disappears under the pile of presents she buys, and she remembers every family birthday with a gift and a check. Her husband, Dennis, is much more conservative and objects to her lavish giving.

Sara says Dennis is "selfish." He calls her "overindulgent and irresponsible." During the thirty-six years they have been married, they have argued more about this issue than about anything else. In recent years, as Dennis has become more concerned about having enough for retirement, their arguments have escalated.

CONFLICTS ABOUT MONEY ARE REALLY CONFLICTING MONEY SCRIPTS

What these two couples don't realize is that their conflicts are actually clashes between the different money scripts they inherited from their families of origin.

In Sam and Eileen's argument over the sports car, Sam's dominant scripts were "I deserve something I really want after all these years of sacrifice" and "It's time to do something I really want to do, for once." Eileen's scripts were "People will think we're self-centered and wasteful," "A car should be practical," and even "Middle-aged men buy sports cars because they're not satisfied with their marriages."

For Sara and Dennis, the conflict over giving to their children and grandchildren also goes back to their own childhoods.

Sara got her first job at age fourteen, and from that time on she received very little support, financial or otherwise, from her family. She formed a money script of "I'm always going to support my children and let them know how much I love them." Ironically, Dennis comes from similar circumstances: he too provided much of his own financial support from the time he was a teenager. He is proud of the self-sufficiency he developed, and one of his primary money scripts is "Giving too much to your children spoils them by encouraging them to be irresponsible."

Identifying money scripts is a crucial first step for couples as well as for individuals in resolving long-standing money conflicts. In previous chapters, we have focused on the value of understanding your own money scripts in order to change the money behaviors that don't serve you well. It is equally valuable to understand your partner's money scripts.

Exploring money scripts as a couple can be a critical step toward developing a healthier financial partnership. When partners recognize each other's money scripts, they can more easily make sense of some of the money behavior on both sides that has brought them into conflict. Besides developing insight into your own history with money and your unconscious beliefs and behaviors, you can develop more understanding and compassion about your partner's money behaviors. This process alone can drastically change the nature of money conflicts. It might not be enough to resolve the conflict, but it can provide an important step toward that resolution.

Research has shown that money is the number one source of conflict in couples, especially early in their marriages. Partners may fight over money, use it to wield power over each other, or keep secrets about it.

Most couples' conflicts over money are really a collision between different sets of money scripts. Each partner has his or her own unique family, work, and relational history with money. As a result, each has a unique set of money scripts. Ironically, we are often drawn to partners who have different money experiences and money scripts, often in an unconscious effort to achieve balance or healing. Spenders find themselves with savers. Someone who is financially disorganized seeks a partner who pays close attention to details. Although these combinations can help both parties to achieve balance, they also set the stage for disagreements.

Sometimes money scripts can reflect habits or assumptions about managing money that the partners learned by watching their parents' interactions. Brenda grew up seeing her mother pay the bills and make most of the day-to-day financial decisions. In her marriage, she assumed that she should do the same. On the other hand, Arturo, her husband, had learned that the man should manage the family money. For this couple, money conflicts were guaranteed.

If you and your partner have different expectations about what constitutes the "normal" way to handle money in a relationship, it is likely to cause conflict. The sad truth is that any discussion of these issues is typically never part of a couple's "getting to know each other" conversations. When these expectations are relatively superficial, simply understanding the source of each other's assumptions can help a couple to develop a workable money-managing system.

Money conflicts that are causing serious problems in the relationship can be much more difficult to resolve. If conflict over money is a reflection of some deeper pathology or difficulties in the relationship, then the couple may require the help of a coach or a therapist. Even for those deeper issues, however, identifying money scripts can help the partners to at least begin to understand each other's behaviors.

FINANCIAL INFIDELITY

Jules, a triathlete, decided that he needed a new bike for his upcoming season of competition. It would cost more than $6,000. He and his wife had agreed not to make major purchases without consulting each other, so he told her about wanting to buy the bike. When she asked him how much it was going to cost, he said, "Twenty-five hundred dollars."

Eventually, after Jules had bought the bike, his wife found out how much it really cost and confronted him about lying to her. He justified his behavior this way: "Well, it was the frame that cost twenty-five hundred dollars. I consider everything else as interchangeable parts, so they weren't exactly part of the bike, and I didn't count them in the purchase price."

Penny never saw a pair of shoes she didn't like. She had hundreds of pairs stacked in boxes in the spare-room closet. Nathan, her husband, finally asked her to talk to him before she bought any more new shoes. She agreed.

In secret, however, Penny kept buying shoes. She would hide them in the back of the closet until she had a chance to put them on and walk up and down the sidewalk, gently scuffing the soles on the concrete. Later, when she showed up wearing the shoes, Nathan might ask, "Are those new shoes?" Without saying a word, she would take off one of the shoes to show him the scuffed sole. Nathan would walk away none the wiser.

Trudy loved antiques, but her husband thought she spent too much on them. To conceal the true cost of the items she bought, she would pay only about half the amount by check. The rest she would pay in cash that she accumulated as she shopped for groceries. She would write checks for twenty dollars more than the cost of the groceries, saving the extra cash until she had enough for her next antiques purchase. Her husband never thought to question the grocery bills. If he complained about the price of an antique, Trudy would show him the check instead of the store receipt that showed the actual purchase price and then show him the appraisal or book value of her latest "great bargain."

Whenever Crystal came home from college for the weekend, she could count on a moment that her dad would find her and surreptitiously slip her a $100 bill, reminding her not to tell her mom.

Patrick's pattern of sexual infidelity was an open secret in his marriage. Every time his wife, Catherine, discovered Patrick's latest fling, she went on a shopping spree. Their unspoken agreement was that if Patrick was going to act out sexually, it was going to cost him.

Is it reasonable to call a lie about buying a new pair of shoes *financial infidelity?* Is keeping secrets from your partner about money okay? Are money secrets innocent deceptions or something more dangerous? Surely withholding the truth from your partner about money isn't in the same category as having an affair.

Perhaps it is not, but it can have the same impact on the ability of partners to trust each other. Partners who lie to each other about finances are certainly not betraying each other sexually, and they would probably not think of their actions as violating their marriage vows or their commitment to the relationship. Nevertheless, keeping money secrets can threaten the very foundation of a relationship.

Financial infidelity includes lying about, hiding, or omitting information about your financial behavior from your partner, especially when the discovery of the secret behavior would result in feelings of guilt or shame. Financial infidelity includes secret spending, secret saving, secret giving, secret borrowing, secret receiving, secret investing, secret gambling, and secret income. Our study did not examine financial infidelity in depth, but we did find the following results:

- On hiding spending from one's family or partner, 15 percent at least "agree a little" that they do so (significantly more women).
- On hiding gambling from people close to them, 1 percent at least "agree a little" that they do so (significantly more men).
- On keeping secrets from one's partner about money, 11 percent at least "agree a little" that it is okay to do so.

ARE YOU GUILTY OF FINANCIAL INFIDELITY?

The following behaviors may constitute financial infidelity:

1. Spending a significant amount from joint funds without first discussing the purchase with your partner. The fact that the lawn tractor is "for both of you" or the suit was "too good a bargain to pass up" doesn't justify making a unilateral decision.

2. Maintaining a secret stash of cash. This might involve physically hiding cash or keeping a separate checking account, savings account, or investment that you hide from your partner.

3. Lying to your partner about the cost of things you purchase. Whether this qualifies as financial infidelity has

nothing to do with the amount involved. Nor does the deception necessarily have to be a direct lie. Penny's non-verbal display of her scuffed soles is just as much a lie as is Jules's misrepresentation of the purchase price of his new bike. The betrayal is in the dishonesty, not the dollar amount or the method of the deceit.

4. Hiding income or assets from your partner. This might include lying about how much you earn, hiding bonuses, being dishonest about your net worth, or accepting secret gifts from parents or other relatives.

5. Overspending and hiding the things you buy from your partner. Both Penny's new shoes and Trudy's "half-priced" antiques are examples of this behavior.

6. Spending money on or giving money to your children (as in Crystal's case) or other relatives without telling your partner. Allowing your children to manipulate you or play one parent against the other is a common aspect of this behavior. Not only is it damaging to the relationship, it also models inappropriate or destructive financial habits to the children.

7. Going to parents, other family members, business partners, banks, or secret credit cards for emergency loans or gifts without discussing the need with your partner. Going over your partner's head in this way is disrespectful and damaging to the relationship. Among other things, it implies that your partner's efforts aren't good enough to

support the family or that you and your partner aren't capable of solving your own financial problems together.

8. Risking joint resources for investments or business purposes without your partner's knowledge or agreement. An example of this might be taking out a second mortgage on your house to buy equipment for your business.

Financial infidelity in a relationship does not suddenly appear out of nowhere. It typically develops over time, and it often grows out of or is part of other problems in the relationship. Like other types of infidelity, it leaves evidence for the partner to find. When the discovery is made, as it most likely will be, the negative fallout is predictable.

These are some of the situations in a relationship that might foster secret spending and financial infidelity:

1. Not talking about money. In order for partners to work together financially, they have to be able to talk about priorities, goals, and difficulties. They have to be able to discuss financial needs. They need to know each other's income, liabilities, and net worth. Otherwise they won't have the resources and information to create and maintain a joint spending plan.

2. One partner choosing to stay ignorant about family finances. This can include signing joint tax returns without looking at them, refusing to have anything to do with balancing checkbooks, letting the other partner take full

responsibility for paying bills, or choosing not to learn about finances. One partner's ignorance or noninvolvement certainly doesn't justify cheating or lying by the other partner. Nevertheless, such passive behavior is an abdication of responsibility. It is refusing to be involved as an equal partner in the financial aspect of the relationship.

3. One partner being a financial bully. If one person tries to control the finances completely or put unreasonable limits on spending, the other partner may feel powerless and see little choice but to hide spending and keep money secrets.

4. A relationship in which one partner is the "parent" and the other is the "child" when it comes to spending. A couple can slip into this pattern particularly easily if one partner is more responsible about money than the other or if one earns or has significantly more money than the other. If one partner thinks it is necessary to monitor the other's spending, or only one of the partners has to ask the other for permission to spend joint funds, they aren't equals when it comes to money. This inequality can foster resentment and lead to secret spending on either side.

5. Closing your eyes to inconsistencies on credit card bills or in bank accounts. Financial infidelity leaves traces. Secret spending has to come from somewhere, and it has to go somewhere. Unexplained cash withdrawals, large credit card balances, or grocery bills that seem unrealistically

high are all possible signs that a partner is spending money
in secret.

6. Choosing not to notice the number of new clothes, electronic gadgets, or household items that mysteriously
appear and seem excessive for the family budget. Even if
your partner shops at Wal-Mart rather than Neiman Mar-
cus, the fact that he or she is bringing home bags and bags
of stuff from every shopping trip means that a serious
amount of money is being spent. The partner who doesn't
seem to pay any attention to all those new possessions
might truly be clueless—or might carefully not be asking
difficult questions that could lead to a painful confronta-
tion about money.

7. Unresolved conflict in a relationship. In a painful relationship, one partner might use spending in an attempt to
"get even" with the other. Spending might also be used as
a way to try to feel better or as a distraction from the
conflict.

Financial infidelity is often tangled up with other difficulties in the relationship, and it almost always will exacerbate
those problems. In many cases, the secret money behavior is
more often the symptom of an underlying problem than the
problem itself.

Obviously, there is a continuum of severity for money
secrets. Forgetting to mention a new pair of earrings is likely to

be less damaging than taking out a secret loan or draining the joint savings account. The more significant the lie, or the more habitual the pattern of lies, the greater the sense of betrayal and the more stress to the partnership.

Nor do all money secrets add up to financial infidelity. Saving on the sly for your partner's birthday gift is very different from lying about the cost of that new computer gadget you just had to have. In addition, it's unreasonable to expect partners to account to each other for every penny they spend. Even when partners manage their money jointly, it is important for both to have personal allowances or separate accounts that they can use in any way they wish.

An important step in dealing with financial infidelity is to learn to distinguish between money secrets that are harmless and those that are destructive. The distinction won't necessarily be the same for everyone. Each couple needs to determine for itself which secrets serve the relationship and which would constitute financial infidelity.

The most important guideline for determining whether a secret is harmful is the intent behind it. Secrets cross the line into infidelity when they are for the purpose of protecting yourself from the consequences of your financial behavior.

CREATING A SAFE FINANCIAL RELATIONSHIP

One way to work toward creating a trusting, safe, honest, and fulfilling financial relationship with your partner is to follow our SAFE plan: speak your truth, agree to a joint money plan, follow the agreement, and establish an emergency response plan.

Speak your truth. Talking about destructive money secrets is the first step toward changing the behavior and healing the relationship. Speaking your truth involves a commitment to being honest with yourself and your partner about your thoughts, feelings, aspirations, and behaviors concerning money. This is far easier said than done. It is easy for us to avoid acknowledging, even to ourselves, our true thoughts and feelings about difficult topics. It is even easier for us to avoid talking about difficult topics with our partners.

Money secrets often grow out of—and also create—deep and painful emotions such as fear, shame, guilt, resentment, and anger. It can be incredibly intimidating to think about acknowledging and talking about those emotions, either your own or those of your partner. Yet doing so is essential if you want to build and maintain a satisfying relationship.

Whether you are beginning to share your own secretive behavior or to confront that of your partner, remember the importance of identifying each other's money scripts as a way of understanding what is behind money secrets.

Speaking your truth includes accepting responsibility for your part in creating the context in which conflict over money arises. Financial problems do not arise in a vacuum, and it has been our experience that *neither party is an innocent bystander.* A crucial component to building a safe relationship is the willingness to accept 100 percent of the responsibility for your 50 percent of the problem. When you use this approach, you no longer feel powerless to change the relationship, because you know that you can do something about your 50 percent.

Agree to a joint money plan. This plan has two essential elements. The first is a plan for working toward a resolution of the money conflicts and issues that are causing problems in your relationship. This can include a commitment to help each other identify money scripts, to work with a financial coach or therapist, and to begin to change problem behavior such as financial infidelity.

The second element is a plan for managing your money. It is important to develop an approach that fits your relationship; there is no one method that is right for every couple. For example, some partners manage all their money and assets jointly, whereas others prefer to keep their funds separate. Either style can work well. We have found, however, two provisions that are especially wise to include in any plan. One is that each partner has a separate amount of money as a personal allowance to spend with complete autonomy and privacy. The second is that each partner agrees not to spend more than a designated amount from the joint funds without consulting the other. Beyond these provisions, a money-management plan should include agreements for creating and following a spending and savings plan, paying off debt, investing for the future, giving to charity, and planning one's estate.

You know you have a good joint money plan when both partners feel like winners and are excited and enthusiastic about what they have created together. If one partner goes into the agreement reluctantly, to please the other, or if the plan is imposed by one partner and the other is resentful, they are setting up their plan to fail. A good money plan allows both partners to be true to themselves—to get their needs met and to feel like equals.

Follow the agreement. An agreement is only as good as a couple's commitment to honoring it and following through with it.

When you create your initial joint money plan, do so with the idea that it is for sixty to ninety days. At the end of that time, review it together. Ask yourselves and each other whether both of you are acting in good faith to keep the spirit as well as the letter of the agreement. If either or both of you are fudging, the plan is not going to work. If one or both of you are having trouble living up to the agreement, the difficulty may lie either with the provisions of the agreement or with the level of commitment to following the plan. Both aspects of the problem may have to be renegotiated in order to build a stronger plan.

An important part of your joint money plan is to create an infrastructure to support both the plan and each of you in following it. That system will usually consist of the following four components:

1. **Actions:** These are specific tasks that you agree to undertake as part of following your plan, such as talking with lenders to arrange debt repayment plans, cutting up credit cards, taking a money-management class, ending behaviors such as "retail therapy" shopping trips or online buying, engaging a financial planner, or seeing a financial counselor or coach.

2. **A support network:** This might include agreeing on a neutral third party such as a financial planner or financial coach to "hold the plan." You also may find it helpful to involve a financial therapist, other couples who are working on financial issues, and other mentors such as business partners or accountants.

3. **Money management tools:** These could include budgeting software, books, classes, or using the services of a bookkeeper or an accountant.

4. **Change tools:** These might be working with a financial counselor or coach, attending workshops to heal money issues, or participating in recovery programs such as Gamblers Anonymous (www.gamblersanonymous.org) or Gam-Anon (www. gam-anon.org).

Establish an emergency response plan. This is an important aspect of each partner's commitment to follow the joint money plan. You increase your chances of having a successful agreement if you plan ahead what you will do if either or both of you can't adhere to the plan, if you want to make changes to the plan, or if the plan fails for any other reason. This also establishes a method of promptly seeking any outside help you might need. Some provisions of an emergency response plan might be as follows:

- Agreeing on a third party (such as a financial therapist) to whom you can go for advice and assistance if you hit a wall
- Agreeing that if one partner thinks the plan is in trouble, the other will cooperate in seeking help
- Agreeing on specific consequences for specific violations of the plan
- Agreeing on rules of engagement (such as the exercise below) for discussing problems

KNEES-TO-KNEES EXERCISE AND NEGOTIATION GUIDELINES

This exercise offers a set of guidelines to help couples discuss challenging problems productively. It can be helpful to use this approach whenever you and your partner need to talk about financial issues that are causing conflict or difficulty in your relationship. The goal is negotiation and compromise.

Remember: Rarely does one partner get everything that he or she wants or needs concerning an issue in a healthy relationship. In the following description, for the sake of clarity, *he* is used for Partner A and *she* is used for Partner B:

1. Partner A identifies an issue and asks Partner B for time to discuss it. They make an appointment and agree to set aside that time without interruption. It is best to keep it simple and focus on one topic at a time. It is also helpful to negotiate how much time to allot to the discussion. If several issues are causing concern, prioritize them before starting the negotiation. Asking for an appointment helps to prevent either partner from feeling blindsided. It also helps each to prepare for the discussion and allows it to take place without distraction. This stands in stark contrast to the way emotionally charged issues are typically discussed in relationships, in which partners ambush each other while they are passing by or avoid talking about the issue at all.

2. Partner A and Partner B sit "knees to knees," facing each other.

3. Each partner does an internal self-check to determine his or her emotions about this issue and the intensity of those feelings on a scale of 1 (low) to 10 (high). If the intensity is 6 or higher for either person, the partners are not ready to discuss the issue. Take time out, usually fifteen to thirty minutes, and reconvene. If at any time during the discussion

one partner reaches 6 or above in intensity, it is time to take a similar break and then return to the discussion. During the break, it is best if the partners do things that are calming in nature rather than ruminate about the issue they are trying to resolve. We further suggest that during the break each person think about something he or she might do differently to move the discussion ahead.

4. Partner A begins with a brief (three to five minutes) presentation of his perspective on the issue. He uses "I" statements and keeps the discussion focused on what he needs regarding the issue and what he is willing to give.

5. Partner A asks Partner B if she needs clarification of his statements. This is not about agreeing or disagreeing with Partner A's perspective; the purpose is to gather information and for Partner B to understand what Partner A has said. Then Partner B uses reflective listening ("What I heard you say is . . . ") to restate what she has heard. If Partner A disagrees with what is reflected, he is given a chance to clarify his intended message.

6. Once both partners have the same understanding of what Partner A has stated, Partner B gives a three- to five-minute presentation of her perspective on the same issue.

7. Reversing roles, the partners repeat step 5.

8. Partner A states one thing he needs from Partner B and one thing he is willing to do to work toward resolution.

9. Partner B listens and clarifies.

10. Partner B can then (a) agree to the proposal, (b) agree to part of the proposal and make a counteroffer ("What I need is . . . and what I'm willing to give is . . . "), or (c) reject the proposal and make a counteroffer.

11. The partners clarify what has been agreed to and write it down before moving on.

12. Once an initial agreement is reached, it is Partner B's turn to state one thing she needs and one thing she is willing to do to work toward resolution.

13. Repeat steps 9 through 11 with Partner B's proposal.

14. Repeat steps 8 through 13 until the issue feels finished or the partners agree to take a break and resume the discussion at a later time. In most cases, it is best not to spend more than about fifteen minutes on an issue; a longer discussion may signal a stalemate or a power struggle. If the partners cannot agree on any part of each other's proposals, stop and agree to try again later, perhaps with the help of a facilitator.

When agreements are reached, do the following:

1. Make commitments *behavioral*. Clarify answers to the questions "How will we know if we are keeping the agreement?" and "What behavior will we see?"

2. Agreements should be time limited. Choose a date for *evaluating* the agreement (usually in thirty, sixty, or

ninety days). Agree to reassess and decide whether to keep, change, or end the agreement.

3. Create a *backup plan* that will be put in place if either or both do not keep the agreement.

4. If appropriate, agree ahead of time on the name of a neutral facilitator to whom both partners agree to be *accountable.*

Here are some additional helpful hints:

1. Check in with feelings whenever necessary and rate them on a scale of 1 (low) to 10 (high).

2. Pause or take time out when feelings intensify to a level of 6 or higher.

3. When the discussion veers off track or either partner feels confused, return to the basics: "What I hear you saying is . . . ," "What I need from you is . . . ," or "What I am willing to give is . . ."

4. Celebrate your agreements and successes.

SHARING DREAMS AND GOALS

For couples, having discussions about money and addressing money-related issues often seems to be synonymous with conflict and difficulty. In order to become full financial partners, it is also important to make time to share your dreams, goals, and successes. Such a process can deepen your intimacy as a couple and help you to support each other in achieving your dreams.

We encourage couples to spend some time reflecting as individuals on their dreams and goals and then sharing them. Completing the "time's up" exercise from the previous chapter is an excellent way to begin this process. You may also find it helpful to use the following prompts:

- What do I love?
- What do we love?
- What and how do we as a couple want to be?
- What are my, your, and our unfulfilled longings?
- What are our individual dreams?
- What are our dreams as a couple?
- What do we want to make sure we accomplish?
- Where would we like to go and what would we like to experience before we die?
- How do we live our life with integrity, consistent with our values?
- What are our regrets?
- Can we do anything about any of those regrets?

We also recommend that once a year you schedule your own private couple's retreat to focus on discussing money as it relates to your goals and visions for the future. This is a time set aside to clarify and talk about your dreams and goals, both individually and as a couple. Then you can develop plans to work together, financially and in other ways, to support those dreams.

CHANGING YOUR MONEY MINDSET: REWIRING MONEY SCRIPTS WITH YOUR PARTNER

Beginning to address money conflicts in a primary relationship takes courage. It demonstrates your commitment, not only to financial health for yourself and your partner but also to the relationship itself.

When you and your partner can increase your understanding of each other's money scripts, you have taken a crucial step toward resolving money issues that threaten your relationship. If the tools in this chapter are used as an ongoing part of your commitment to resolving those issues, they can help you to heal those issues. As you build a healthier financial partnership, you will also help each other to create a more fulfilling, richer life together.

CHAPTER TEN

—◦•◦—

RAISING FINANCIALLY
HEALTHY CHILDREN

*A*s *you begin to examine* your money scripts, including those that have been passed down from generation to generation, it becomes increasingly clear just how much power these family money scripts can have. Just as your parents' money scripts, spoken and unspoken, were passed down to you, you will pass your money scripts on to your own children.

Among the benefits of creating financial health for yourself is the opportunity to pass that health along to your children and grand-children. It is possible to interrupt generational cycles of destructive financial behavior and teach your children more balanced ways to deal with money.

If you don't have children of your own, you may still find the information in this chapter to be useful in further under-standing the origins of your own money scripts. It is also important to keep in mind that even if you are not a parent, you are one of the financial role models for any children who are part of your life.

WHAT YOU DO SPEAKS LOUDER
THAN WHAT YOU SAY

Perhaps the single most important thing you can do to help teach your children more balanced money behavior is to create financial health for yourself. With money, as with anything else, children learn far more from watching what you do than from hearing what you tell them. Identifying and rewiring your own problematic money scripts and engaging in healthy financial behaviors are the best ways to help your children's healthy financial development. Model for your children the money behavior you want them to learn.

Understanding your money scripts can give you a great deal of insight into some of the interactions, issues, and chronic conflicts about money that you may have with your children. Doug, for example, grew up hearing from his parents and his grandmother, "You should be grateful to have something to eat and a roof over your head. If you want anything extra, you have to earn it."

When he was eight years old, Doug lied about his age to get his first job, delivering papers. Forty years later, he was still working hard. He had become financially successful, and he was still following his family money script of "If you want anything extra, you have to earn it." Doug and his wife could easily afford to give their two daughters whatever they needed and wanted, and Doug wanted the girls to have an easier childhood than he had had. At the same time, his money script said his children should have to work for what they got.

With this unresolved internal conflict, Doug was inconsistent with his daughters, alternating between indulgent giving and saying no even to reasonable requests. He expected them to earn their allowances and comfortable lifestyle, not directly by working for money but by getting good grades, being obedient, and behaving well.

For Doug, coming to terms with and rewiring this core money script was an important step in creating more balance with his daughters about money. As he gained insight into his own behavior, Doug began to work with his wife to provide more consistent and balanced expectations for the girls.

WHAT YOU DON'T TEACH YOUR CHILDREN ABOUT MONEY, SOCIETY WILL

Our culture is in a destructive trance about money. Despite historically high debt rates, bankruptcy rates, foreclosures, debt delinquencies, and financial stress, we just keep right on spending. We try to keep up with the Joneses, not recognizing that the Joneses are neck deep in debt and on the brink of losing their home and having their brand new Cadillac Escalade repossessed. Our children watch the modern versions of the television show *Lifestyles of the Rich and Famous*, including *Platinum Weddings, My Super Sweet Sixteen,* and *Cribs,* which teach them that the one with the most expensive parties, homes, and toys wins.

A crucial factor in raising financially healthy children is to accept that part of being a parent is counteracting these harmful messages and teaching your children about money. This can be tougher than it sounds. Many of us try to avoid thinking about money ourselves, especially the uncomfortable reality of our own financial situation. In addition, we are not taught to talk about money and in fact are instructed not to do so. However, learning how to manage money is an essential life skill, just like learning to drive, cook, or do laundry. As parents, we wouldn't even think of putting our teenagers behind the wheel of a car without some serious instruction. Yet it doesn't necessarily occur to us that it's just as unreasonable—and every bit as dangerous—to send them out to handle their first paychecks without any guidance.

Once again, regardless of whether you consciously make an effort to teach your children about money, the home is the primary place they will learn their lessons. If you have an unbalanced relationship with money, you will be modeling the same for your children. If you are stuck in a particular financial comfort zone, without outside help or influence, your children are likely to limit themselves in a similar fashion. They learn by example, not lecture. After all, even though they may not show it, they think you are cool and want to grow up to be just like you.

Schools do only a limited amount of instruction about finances, much of it coming long after the students' money scripts are solidly in place. Many of the money messages from our consumerist society are unhealthy ones, amounting to countless repetitions of "buy this," "you must have that," and "everyone needs these." These messages must be counteracted by you if they are not to be internalized.

THE VALUE OF STRUGGLE

The story is told of a child watching a butterfly labor to emerge from its cocoon. Feeling sorry for the creature and wanting to end its struggle, the child tears open the cocoon to set the butterfly free. The butterfly flaps its wings, flutters a few feet, and tumbles to the ground. Denied the effort of working its way out of the cocoon, the butterfly lacks the strength it needs to use its wings and survive on its own.

In much the same way, you deprive your children of essential strength when you interfere with the struggles that teach them the connection between their behavior and its consequences in the world. Since children are sheltered from many of these natural consequences (at least for a while), it is up to parents to artificially create consequences so children can learn. Rescuing children from feeling the discomfort associated with poor decisions stunts their learning and their growth. These are lessons they will need to learn at some point, and it's far better for them to do so when the consequences are childhood disappointments rather than adult dilemmas. The meaning of money and one's appropriate relationship with it is one of the important things that parents have the opportunity to teach their children.

As a parent, you want the best for your children. However, giving them whatever they want is not necessarily giving them the best. Some of the most damaging money lessons you can teach your children are (1) that they can have anything they want and don't have to earn it through behaving well, doing chores, or doing well in school, and (2) that you will always bail them out financially.

If you want to create an environment that will help your children to grow up to be financially healthy adults, here are some suggestions.

Set limits and stick by them. One of the biggest mistakes parents make is not setting limits with their children. For example, if you give your children allowances, be clear up front about what those allowances are supposed to cover. Then make sure you abide by your own rules.

Ten-year-old Clarissa was expected to save part of her allowance for any special toys she wanted. One day when she was at the mall with her mom, Clarissa saw the latest and greatest "must-have" electronic gizmo. It was on sale, but she didn't have the money to buy it because she hadn't been saving. Her mom gave in to Clarissa's begging and bought it for her. Mom did avoid upsetting her daughter, who would have thrown a fit and "hated" her for half a day, but she didn't do Clarissa a favor in the long run. Instead, she taught Clarissa a lasting lesson: lobby hard enough and you will get what you want, whether or not it is the appropriate thing. Experiencing her mother saying no, on the other hand, would have helped Clarissa to remember that when her money was gone, it was gone, and maybe next time she would do better at setting aside some money as savings.

Enforce and allow consequences. One benefit of giving children a chance to make money choices is that it allows them to experience the consequences when the stakes are small. This is one of the wisest things you can do as a parent to teach your children about money. If a twelve-year-old isn't able to buy a video game he wants, because he has developed the habit of spending all his allowance immediately, the experience can provide a valuable lesson in the importance of saving. It may be painful at the time, but it's far less painful than the experience, ten years later, of not being able to pay his rent because he has spent his weekly paychecks as fast as he got them. Rest assured, this is a lesson he will need to learn. It is up to you, to a large degree, whether your child learns these lessons in the safety of childhood or as an adult, when the stakes are much higher.

Don't underestimate children's competence. Children who are old enough to receive allowances are old enough to understand more than you might think about how money works. Instead of brushing aside your children's questions about money decisions, give them age-appropriate explanations.

As parents, work together. Isaac often goes shopping with his dad on Saturday mornings. They frequently stop at the local

candy shop to have a treat. Dad has given Isaac strict instructions: "Don't ever tell your mom about this, or we won't be able
to do it."

This kind of collusion and secret-keeping, which is especially
common when parents are divorced, teaches children to be
manipulative and to play one parent against the other. Giving
children money behind the other parent's back, or interfering
with consequences the other parent is trying to enforce, damages both the parents' relationship with each other and the
child's relationship with money. It is essential for parents to
work out between themselves any differences they may have
over children and money, so they can work as a team when they
are with the child. If they don't, their children are more likely
to grow up to keep secrets about their own money behaviors,
even while professing honesty in relationships.

ONE FAMILY'S APPROACH

Bill and Carol Stough were gracious enough to share with
us their approach to teaching their son, Alex, and daughter,
Lindsay, about money and to give us permission to use their
real names. The Stoughs' method directly contradicts one of
the top ten money scripts: "It's not nice (or necessary) to talk
about money." Instead, their philosophy might be summarized
as "It's essential to talk about money with your children."

As an accountant and a financial advisor, Bill has learned from his clients that one of the biggest mistakes families make is keeping money matters a secret. He and his wife have chosen to be open with their children about money. Their children know the family's income and net worth. They are included in major financial decisions and in working toward the family's long-term financial goals.

The seven essential components of the Stoughs' approach to raising financially healthy children are described below.

Talk openly about money. Money is not a taboo topic in the Stough household. Lindsay and Alex are not only allowed to ask questions about money matters, they are encouraged to do so. They are involved in discussions about major purchases, which has helped them to learn about comparison shopping, using credit wisely, and doing research before making decisions. When it comes to finances, Bill says, "Kids have a billion questions and no one to ask." He and his wife make sure that they are available to answer those questions.

Bill and Carol take advantage of opportunities to teach their children how money works. For example, Alex, a musician, has a valuable violin. When it was damaged recently, Bill had Alex participate in submitting a claim to the insurance company and getting the instrument repaired. It was a chance for him to learn how insurance works and about its value in protecting expensive possessions.

Give children opportunities to make their own decisions

and their own mistakes. Alex and Lindsay are allowed to choose what to spend or save from their allowances (which are modest) and any money they receive as gifts. They are encouraged to find their own balance and to realize that it's possible to save and spend at the same time, depending on your choices.

Provide incentives to encourage wise money behavior. Carol and Bill match, dollar for dollar, any funds the children add to their savings accounts. Their intent is not only to encourage immediate savings but also to show their son and daughter the value of taking advantage of opportunities, such as 401(k) savings plans, that offer employer matching.

Plan for the future. The day after their wedding, Bill and Carol put some of the money they had received as wedding gifts into a college savings account—for children who hadn't been born yet. They continued to make regular contributions to it over the years. Now that Lindsay and Alex are teenagers, their college accounts are sufficient to pay for undergraduate degrees at excellent schools.

Their parents have made clear that when the college fund is gone, it's gone. Alex and Lindsay will be responsible for any costs over and above the amounts in their college funds. If they budget wisely and don't spend the entire fund, however, they get to keep whatever is left. Once they graduate, any remaining money is theirs to use in any way they wish. Lindsay, at fourteen years old, has already figured out that if she gets a full scholarship, she will have an impressive graduation gift.

Live on less than you make. The Stoughs believe in being humble about what money you do have or make, that it's not how much you make but how much you spend that matters. They could live more lavishly than they do, but they aren't fans of conspicuous consumption. They are teaching their children by example that giving is a key use of money. They understand that debt has its place but should be used cautiously. They use credit cards as a convenience only, never as a source of daily living expenses, and they pay off debts as fast as possible. Bill's expression is that people who have cars, houses, and toys they can't comfortably afford are "leasing their lives." Even though Carol and Bill are open with their children about their net worth and their income, they have also told Lindsay and Alex that they trust them to keep that information private. They don't believe that financial status should be a matter of competition.

Set goals and make conscious choices about your financial resources in order to support those goals. Bill and Carol came into their marriage with compatible financial outlooks, and they set financial goals from the beginning. This allowed them to set an overall tone for their family's financial future and to bring their children into the process later. An early goal was for Bill to invest in further education and get his MBA. By helping him to advance in his career and increase his earnings, this allowed the Stoughs to achieve a second goal: allowing Carol to leave her job and be home with the children. A current goal is for Bill to be able to retire from full-time work in a few years, when he turns fifty.

Achieving these goals has taken discipline, commitment, and an understanding of the value of delayed gratification. It is one of the reasons the Stoughs have chosen to live modestly and use their financial resources conservatively. At the same time, they have not focused on future goals at the expense of enjoying life in the present. They take family vacations, for example, but they balance a major vacation, like a trip to Alaska, with a more modest vacation, like a camping trip, the following year. Decisions about expenditures such as vacations are made as a family, with the children understanding the trade-offs because they are fully involved in working toward the family goals.

It is also worth noting that providing for their own financial security is as important to Bill and Carol as providing for their children's education. They started investing for their own retirement at the same time they started saving for college, keeping those funds separate.

Teach by example. When Lindsay was six years old, she was in the grocery store with her mother one day and picked a bag of candy off the shelf. She took it to Carol and asked, "Is this on sale, and can we buy it?"

Even at that young age, she understood from watching her parents shop that the way to buy groceries was to pay attention to what was on sale. For the Stoughs, thrift is a well-developed family habit and a core value. The children have learned and accepted that value for themselves, in large part by observing and being part of what their parents do.

Bill and Carol emphasize the value of having children understand the process and the reasons behind money behavior. When children see the why and how of parents' money choices, much of the conflict between parents and children over money is eliminated. Fairness is also important. Children can accept no as an answer for themselves much more readily when they see parents also saying no to themselves.

Bill sums up his and Carol's way of teaching their children about money this way: "Show them what you do and why, and let them have some say."

IT IS NEVER TOO LATE TO START OVER

It is never too late to affect your children in a positive way. Any positive changes you make can influence them for the better, whether they are minors or adults. Children learn by example, and they can continue to learn from you as adults. As your relationship with money improves, you can serve as a resource to assist them in gaining financial knowledge, challenging dysfunctional money scripts, and learning healthy financial behaviors.

If, unlike the Stoughs, you realize that you are making or have made more than a few mistakes with your children (young or adult) regarding money, here are some tips that have worked for other clients of ours:

1. If you are brave, sit down with your children and tell them you have discovered that you have been doing some things with money that are not in your and their best interests and that you will be making some changes in your behavior.

2. If you are not that brave, have the same conversation whenever the opportunity to act in the old ways comes up. Let them know that you now realize your previous actions have been mistaken and that you don't want to keep making the same mistakes. Admit that you have been wrong, rather than blaming them for continuing to expect you to act in the ways you have taught them to expect.

3. Tell them how your thinking has changed and how things are going to work differently in the future.

4. Be prepared for your children to resist your new behavior. Get support from others who understand what you are trying to do. Unless you are really lucky, the pressure to go back to the way it has always been will be incredible. If you have helped to create a well-established pattern of financial enabling or other damaging money behavior, it may be valuable to seek help from a financial planner, coach, or therapist. If you have difficulty saying no, sometimes you can have your financial planner do it for you.

When you let your children know that you have been wrong and you intend to change your behavior, you are teaching them an important lesson: it is okay to make mistakes, and admitting those mistakes and then correcting the behavior is what responsible adults do when it's necessary.

Lucie's mom didn't want her four-year-old daughter to have candy. Despite knowing this, Lucie's grandmother secretly brought Lucie a bag of candy every time she visited, hiding the pieces in various places around the house. It was a secret little "candy game" that Grandma and Lucie played, with the rule being to make sure that Mommy didn't find out. Grandma thought of it as just an innocent, endearing game between the two of them.

One day, while talking with a friend about integrity and how important it was to her, Lucie's grandma realized she was not practicing integrity with her own daughter. She realized that what she was doing was teaching her granddaughter—at age four—to lie and be deceitful to her mom.

Shortly after Grandma arrived on her next visit, Lucie came up to her and whispered, "Are we playing our candy game, Grandma?"

Grandma said, "You know, darling, it isn't right for us to keep secrets from your mommy. I'm sorry I asked you to do it. That isn't a good game, and we aren't going to play it anymore."

Lucie's response was "Whew, Grandma, that game made me so nervous. I'm glad we won't play it anymore."

David and Melanie had financially supported their four adult children for decades. They would make house payments for them, pay for private schools for the grandchildren and support their extracurricular activities, pay utility bills, pay tax bills, and pay off bad loans. This financial enabling was beginning to threaten their own retirement.

Eventually, at the urging of their financial planner, they sought help from a therapist who helped them to get over what they discovered was their unconscious guilt about not having been the parents they wished they had been when their children were growing up. She helped them to understand that they had been giving financially to their children in an attempt to make up for their earlier mistakes. After working with the therapist for several months, David and Melanie scheduled a family meeting. They told their children they realized that what they had been doing, in an attempt to be of help, had actually been destructive. They told them that over the next six months they would be reducing their financial support, and within a year they would be stopping altogether.

Predictably, this did not go over well. The meeting dissolved into chaos, tears, and shouting. As hard as it was to do, David and Melanie held to their new position. They offered to pay for several family sessions with their therapist and their financial planner to help everyone come to terms with the changes. Reluctantly, the children agreed to participate.

The next year was a difficult time of conflict and tension for the whole family. Eventually, however, David and Melanie's commitment to healthier financial behavior began to bear fruit. As the children were required to take full financial responsibility for themselves, they began to realize their own competence and take pride in their self-reliance. In addition, as they came to understand the damaging effect of their parents' financial enabling, they started to change their behavior with their own children. The result was a shift toward more balanced money beliefs and actions that created healthier relationships with money for three generations.

CHANGING YOUR MONEY MINDSET: TEACHING HEALTHIER MONEY BEHAVIOR TO YOUR CHILDREN

What are some of the money messages you have given your children, both directly and through your actions? Which messages have been less healthy than you would wish? How would you like to change what you do with your children concerning money? Remember that it's never too late to begin doing something different. You don't have to change everything at once; beginning with small steps can eventually make a big difference. Changing damaging behaviors with money, especially when those behaviors involve other people, is not easy. It can be done, however, and it is well worth the effort it requires.

Creating a healthier relationship with money can have a powerful impact not only on your own life but also on the lives of your children and grandchildren.

CHAPTER ELEVEN

CHANGE YOUR MONEY MINDSETS AND CREATE THE LIFE YOU WANT

A s people come to know better, they can do better. We hope that from what you have read and the exercises you have done in the process of reading this book, you now have information and tools that can help you to change the behaviors that are the most troubling for you.

The change process we describe does work. We've witnessed it in our own lives, in the lives of our clients, and in the research we have conducted. We do not believe that anyone is terminally unique. The chances are that we've heard some version of your story before. You are not so much worse off than or so different from others who have been able to transform their financial lives by changing their money mindsets. Take heart from the fact that you can create a different life for yourself from this day forward.

Creating that different life will take courage. Certainly, you will need knowledge as you begin to integrate these new principles into your life, but we suspect that you will need more courage than knowledge. This is because it takes effort to change. For most of us, there is no instant transformation. Lasting change takes time, effort, and commitment. When you begin putting your changes into action, you may have to start doing things differently from the way your family and friends do them. As you begin to test the outer limits of your financial comfort zone, others may begin to feel uncomfortable with your new behaviors. It will take persistence and courage to sustain your new path to wealthier thinking and living.

To put what you have learned into action, we leave you with seven steps to make your transition to a new life easier.

SEVEN WAYS TO PUT YOUR NEW MONEY MINDSETS INTO MOTION

Believe you can have what you want. You *can* have more of what you want than you ever imagined. As you may recall, in our research we found that the wealthy believe they deserve money. The most important difference between those who achieve their goals and those who are not happy with their lot in life involves the degree to which they believe it is possible for them to get what they want in the first place. High achievers are utterly convinced that they can meet or surpass their goals. Low achievers are equally certain that they cannot; as a result, they often avoid setting goals in the first place. Since your thoughts define and reinforce your reality, both ways of thinking prove right in the end. It might not be easy to shake self-limiting beliefs, but they are the only true barrier to achievement. We invite you to decide to live in a world where it is possible for you to reach your goals.

To believe you can have what you want, you first need to know what it is you really want. We've given you a number of exercises to help you drill down to the core needs or desires that underlie those on the surface. You may say you want a red

Mercedes, but the underlying desire is actually to have more fun in your life. Perhaps you say you want a flat in London, when really what you want is more intellectual stimulation and challenge. Start first by becoming aware of what it is you really want. Who knows, you might already have some of it right now.

Since you can have more of whatever you want, shoot for the moon. Many people will encourage you to set only "reasonable" or "realistic" goals, perhaps because they don't want you to feel hurt or disappointed if you fail to achieve them. However, we challenge you to set some outrageous goals as well. If the highest achievers got that way by challenging the perceived limits of possibility, should you trust only what you or your friends think is reasonable? The most notable men and women in history vigorously embraced "impossible" goals— and the rest of the world got in line and conformed to fit their reality. Save the reasonable and realistic goals as action steps that move you toward the fulfillment of your big dreams.

Erika had a dream of owning her own dental practice in her small midwestern hometown. The real challenge wasn't that Erika was too young, which she was, or that she didn't have enough money, which she didn't. The biggest challenge was that Erika wasn't even a dentist. Ever since graduating from college, Erika had worked at a job that paid well but that she didn't enjoy. She saved everything she could for three years, then, with the help of student loans, enrolled in dental school. On graduating, she found a position in a dental clinic in her town. Although she had moved very close to realizing her dream, this was still not it.

Within one year of moving back to her hometown, a most amazing opportunity came Erika's way. A long-established dentist decided to retire and wanted to sell his practice. She engaged a financial planner to analyze the deal. He assured her that the practice was a great opportunity and helped her to find a company that specialized in making loans on dental practices. She was able to borrow 99 percent of the money she needed to buy not only the practice but also the building it occupied. Today, Erika owns her dream practice in her hometown. She is thirty-one years old.

Passion-test your goals. If you are not 100 percent in love with a goal, take some time to evaluate whether it is really your goal after all. If you experience any hesitation, the chances are good that it might not be what you really want, or it might be someone else's goal for you. We call these "should goals," and they are very different from authentic goals. Authentic goals fill us with passion and energy, inspire those around us, and may even keep us up at night because we are too excited to sleep. If you do not feel this way about your goal, consider letting go of it. Until you become honest and real, you will not be able to discover and awaken your true passion.

Colin's grandfather was a doctor, his father was a doctor, his older sister was a nurse, and his older brother was a counselor.

Everyone in the family, including Colin, assumed that he would follow the family tradition and go into the health field. During college, Colin had a part-time job as an emergency medical technician and ambulance driver. In addition to enjoying the satisfaction of helping people, he loved the adrenaline rush of emergency calls and ambulance runs. His enjoyment of his job seemed to reinforce his decision to become an emergency room physician.

Then Colin flunked chemistry—three times. He hated the class, and he simply couldn't force himself to concentrate enough to make sense of it. When he looked at the long list of science classes between him and his goal of becoming a doctor, he felt sick. There was no way, he decided. Medicine simply wasn't for him. Discouraged and feeling as if he were letting down the entire family, Colin was ready to drop out of school completely.

Fortunately, he talked to a career counselor with the training and the wisdom to help him uncover his true passion. Helping people mattered greatly to Colin; medicine didn't. The lengthy education and painstaking attention to detail that being a doctor required didn't fit him at all. What he really loved most about his job was the drama and excitement of helping people in crisis situations. Eventually, Colin left the university and enrolled in a firefighting program at a technical school. It took courage for him to explain his wishes to his family, and it took some time for them to accept his choice. However, Colin's passion for his chosen field eventually won them over, and after fifteen years as a firefighter he still loves every day of his job.

Write down your goals. There is tremendous power in taking the time to put your goals down on paper, even if you never look at the paper again. Doing so helps you to gain clarity and vision. It is an important step in making your thoughts a reality, and it offers an inspiring record of the power of the goal-setting process.

One New Year's Day, James wrote out a long list of goals. Some of them were in line with his current career and relationship paths, but a few were "outrageous" goals. One day, several years later, James was sorting through some paperwork in preparation for a move. He found his list of goals, which he had forgotten he had even made. As he read through the list, James found his eyes filling with tears of amazement and gratitude. He had achieved almost every goal on the list. Such is the power of writing down your goals.

We encourage you to set goals and review them at least yearly. If you need additional resources on how to uncover your authentic goals, how to distinguish them from "should goals," and how action steps differ from goals, we encourage you to use the process outlined in our previous book, *The Financial Wisdom of Ebenezer Scrooge: 5 Principles to Transform Your Relationship with Money.*

Visualize yourself in the process of achieving your goals. Notice that we said "in the process of." It is important to distinguish between visualizing the *process* of goal achievement and visualizing the *outcome* of goal achievement. Researchers Lien Pham and Shelley Taylor from the University of California researched this distinction and found some surprising results. It turns out that we are much more likely to achieve our goals if we visualize ourselves taking the steps to achieve them rather than visualizing ourselves already having achieved them. In fact, they found that you are better off not visualizing at all than focusing on the outcome. This finding flies in the face of what most self-help books teach.

The value of visualizing the process of achieving goals makes sense. For example, let's say you are a tennis player and your goal is to win a local tournament. Spending time visualizing yourself performing good footwork, hitting solid shots, rotating your trunk on your backhand, and using good follow-through will stimulate your brain to rehearse these actions. Research has found that when such visualization is done properly, the brain doesn't distinguish between performing an action and mentally rehearsing it. As a result, this process of visualization will increase your ability to perform the action. However, if you spend all your time visualizing yourself receiving the trophy, the crowds applauding as you win, and the joy you will feel, your visualization will not help you to prepare. In fact, it might hurt you by making you become overconfident.

Therefore, when you visualize, picture yourself carrying out the actions that will help you along the way to achieving your goals. Close your eyes. What do you see? Where are you? What are you doing? Who is with you? How does it feel? Breathe it in. Take a few moments each day to make the vision of you in the process of achieving your goals come to life in the stillness of your mind.

Brian and DeAnn had discussed a number of times throughout the twenty years of their marriage that they should probably start putting together a plan for the later years of their lives. They would go through long periods of not doing anything. At other times, Brian would unsuccessfully try to get DeAnn to go with him to talk to a financial planner, or DeAnn would try unsuccessfully to convince Brian to go with her. Nothing happened.

When discussing this situation one day with a friend, DeAnn realized that both she and Brian had no personal clear picture of what they would be planning. That night when she returned home, she sat down with Brian and had him tell her how he would like life to be, if they could live it in any way they wanted. She shared what her ideal situation would be. They both realized that with just a little planning, all that they wanted was possible.

Almost as if by magic, Brian agreed to call a friend to get a referral for helping them to come up with a plan. DeAnn didn't have to be coaxed or coerced to attend the meeting. It was with a lot of excitement and anticipation that they met with their new advisor. Within days they had collected all the information he needed. In the next seven years they saved and invested every cent they could. As they got closer to their goal, the excitement built and increased their motivation. Now retired, they are living their dreams. The simple, powerful act of grasping their vision and allowing themselves to move toward it enabled them to live as no one else in their respective families had ever done.

Break down bigger goals into smaller, manageable steps, but keep the primary goal in mind. Researchers have found that focusing too much on the success of achieving subgoals or action steps can distract or discourage you from taking further steps toward achieving your primary goal. This is because your action steps are rarely as exciting as your ultimate goal. You may have a goal, as Erika did, to become a dentist. Although that goal has a lot of passion, filling out the application to dental school and meeting the deadline is not exactly what you dream about. However, it's a necessary step that will move you toward that big goal. Also, if you put too much effort into celebrating your smaller achievements along the way, you will be less motivated to continue moving forward. Frequently visualizing yourself in the process of achieving your goals will help you to always keep your ultimate goal in mind while you are moving forward.

Find others who support your goals. Get a goal buddy (or buddies). Share your goals with each other. Identify some specific action steps you will take each week to move forward, and report to each other on your progress. If your goal buddy doesn't think your goal is reasonable or possible to achieve, find a new goal buddy.

Surround yourself with an appropriate support team. This could include a financial mentor, a financial planner, an investment advisor, a financial therapist, a financial coach, an accountant, an attorney, a banker, a bookkeeper, and an insurance broker. You probably won't need all these professionals, but you will need some of them.

You can find listings of financial planners and financial therapists who work with clients' money scripts at www.wisdomofscrooge.com. If reading this book has helped you to identify money disorders such as compulsive spending or compulsive gambling, you may also find it valuable to participate in a support group such as Debtors Anonymous (www.debtorsanonymous.org) or Gamblers Anonymous (www.gamblersanonymous.org).

Putting these seven principles into practice will unlock your passion and open doors you never knew existed. The transformation will not take place overnight, but when you commit to change, you may be astonished at how quickly you can create the abundant, fulfilling life you have always wanted.

INDEX

Page numbers followed by an *f* indicate figures.

NOTES

NOTES